You Laugh, I'll Drive

Giving Yourself the Green Light to Enjoy
Life — Speed Bumps and All — and Stop
Worrying About Your Mile(age)!

by Jenny Herrick

with Kathy Hoeschen Massey

First Printing, July 2007
Second Printing, February 2009

Visit Jenny Herrick's website at www.allkiddingaside.biz
or e-mail her at: jenny@allkiddingaside.biz.

"You Laugh, I'll Drive" by Jenny Herrick
with Kathy Hoeschen Massey.

ISBN: 978-0-9794317-0-8

Published by All Kidding Aside, Sioux City, IA. Cover and text
printed by Pacific City Graphics, South Sioux City, Nebraska.

Cover Design: Eve Sides, Dakota City, Nebraska, and Kathy
Hoeschen Massey, Sioux City, Iowa.

Dedication

I dedicate this book to my three children
— Kirk, Eric and Jana —
in thanks for providing me with
so much material;
to my assistant, Marge,
for always having just what I need
up her sleeve;
and to my many friends
who never leave home
without their red noses.

Acknowledgements

Thank you to my audience members who stimulated me to even think about writing a book. If it hadn't been for you, I wouldn't have put my stories down on paper.

To my terrific Toastmaster friends — without you and our great organization, I wouldn't have pursued my speaking career and without your guidance, encouragement and challenges, I wouldn't be where I am today in my business.

Thanks to my new friends in the National Speakers Association, especially Kate Adamson, who is always only a phone call away when I need advice on how to self-publish a book.

To Marge, my traveling companion, trusty assistant and genuine friend. I can always count on you (which I definitely do often)! You are one in a million.

God bless my daughter-in-love, Sandi Martin who IS good enough for my baby boy, who never gets tired of listening to me, always knows just the right words to soothe, smooth and stroke my ego...what a gift you are to me! Love you, San.

To my Kennel Club friends . . .dog people are MY kind of people! I know I speak for them when I say "I hope when I die, it's with a good dog on the end of the leash!"

To my Mastermind group, who are hard taskmasters — which I definitely need or I'd still be back in the "I think I should write a book" stage — thanks for your insight, advice and your patience in putting up with me.

Thanks to my special workplace pal, Janet Adam, who taught me so much! Little important things ... such as how to tie a silk scarf around my neck for the ultimate finishing touch to an outfit; the correct way to put eye liner on; when it was appropriate to roll sleeves up and when it wasn't. Janet, I can still hear you saying: "If you want to look casual, go ahead and roll them up, but if you want to look *professional,* leave them down." Thanks, dear friend, you are my role model!

A special thanks also to my friend, Dot, who calls and says: "I need a Jenny hit!" Oh, how we *all* need to feel needed!

And I can't forget my funny friends with grease paint on their faces, frizzy hair on their heads and oversized shoes on their feet.... Do a good job at my funeral, I'm countin' on you!

I can't tell you how many times I've heard the phrase "Everyone has a book in them." My deepest thanks and gratitude to Kathy Hoeschen Massey who helped me get that book out! For your expertise with the written word and creative ability to take my stories and make such perfect sense out of them, while we're both laughing all the way, Kathy . . . you ROCK!!

…and finally and most importantly, to my Heavenly Father whom I know loves me and always will.

Chapter	Page

1. Hold On, It's Going to Be a Bumpy Ride! 2
2. Crank Up the Attitude! 5
3. We've All Got to Start Somewhere 10
4. Should Have Stopped With the First One 14
5. Fear of the Lord ... and My Mother.............................. 17
6. School Daze 20
7. Three Tough Years 23
8. A Good Trade 26
9. A Whistle and a Prayer....................................... 31
10. One Last Kiss 34
11. Saying Goodbye and Looking Ahead 37
12. Returning to the Nest 41
13. Little House on Cypress Street................................ 47
14. When All Else Fails, Get a Puppy!............................ 52
15. Head 'Em Up, Move 'Em Out, Rawhide 58
16. Went in for a Horse, Came Out With a Husband........... 61
17. It's Now or Never.. 64
18. Sons are Sons 'til They Take a Wife,
    But Daughters Stick Around to Run Your Life! 66
19. No Strangers, Just Friends I Haven't Yet Met 70
20. Choose to Love Your Job or Choose a Different Job......... 74
21. Never Too Old to Go Pro 81
22. Can You Come Out and Play? 84
23. Keep Talking, God, I'm Trying to Listen! 86
24. Not the Sharpest Crayon, But I Am Pretty Colorful 92
25. Breaking the Language Barrier with Laughter.............. 98
26. Face to Face, Halfway Across the World................... 104
27. Then Came 9/11 108
28. Don't Worry, Caden, I Will! 114
29. Hey, It's My Funeral.......................................118
30. A Few Last Thoughts Before I Pull Over
    And Let You Out 120

> *The constitution only gives people*
> *the right to* pursue *happiness.*
> *You have to catch it yourself.*
> ~ Benjamin Franklin

1
Hold On, It's Going to be a Bumpy Ride

I've got a lot of miles on me, and believe me — they're not all the pretty, scenic, feel-the-breeze-in-your-face and smell-that-beautiful-air-type miles.

Some of them are more like the "omigosh what IS that SMELL?" kind of miles. Or the "that is one nasty piece of road kill" miles. Or the "why didn't I stop and ask for directions!?!" kind of miles.

This road trip I call my life hasn't all been smooth asphalt. Speed bumps, detours, head-on collisions? I've seen them all. Yet somehow — by the grace of God, sheer, dumb luck and the realization that when it's "sink-or-swim" time, I'm pretty darn good at dog-paddling — I'm here to tell you about it. Because while nobody ever said life was going to be easy, I say that peeking at someone else's road map can make it a little easier to avoid some of the potholes.

The person I am today is stronger than I ever imagined I could be, spiritually, emotionally and any other way I can think of that a person can be strong! Strong-smelling, even! OK, but that's only when I get home from power-walking the dog.

In sharing my story, I hope to help you to accelerate through rough spots in your road, and perhaps provide you with the tools to detour around a tough situation. After all, I've developed a few coping tools on my trip.

The most important tool? A sense of humor. A sense of humor is more than just the shine on your chassis; it's the oil in your engine! It's that "oomph" you get when you "floor it" on the interstate! Being able to laugh at life and find joy on even the darkest days is key to not only surviving, but thriving on this amazing road trip called life!

Bringing a smile to your face — or perhaps even a laugh to your voice — is what I also want to do as I add in brief "rest stops" along the way in this book. I hope you enjoy the little side comments, quotes and jokes. Where I know the source, I have cited it; where I don't know the source, it's just a little gem I've collected on my journey. Either way, I hope you enjoy the little distractions. I know that they keep me laughing.

To me, laughing is as important as breathing. Some days, I can't go more than a minute without doing one or the other.

And my favorite kind of laughter is that deep, hearty belly laugh that can literally take your breath away!

But be careful — laughing that hard while driving could cause serious injury! So sit back, buckle up, and let me do the driving for a little while....

> Think of laughter as *inner aerobics!* Laughter can improve your circulation and strengthen your heart, and it's a lot more fun than hanging out in a stinky ol' gym!

Me in one of my favorite spots — on the podium, speaking to "anyone who'll listen!"

*Don't be afraid that your life will end,
be afraid that it will never begin.*

~ Anonymous

2
Crank Up the Attitude!

*D*o you know that some people just don't have IT?
And when I say "IT," I mean that all-important *sense
of humor.*

How sad! That's like being born without a funny bone. Without a funny bone, you couldn't bend your elbow. And then
how would you scratch your nose or other important, often-
itchy body parts?

Let's back up…. Research studies have shown there are
people who are "humor impaired" (whatever that means).
My guess is they're describing people who are unable to
laugh at the obvious, unable to see the "funny" in situations,
unable to enjoy their days a little more through the use of

their sense of humor. They wouldn't know witty if it landed on their lunch.

You might know persons like that. Pity them.

Attitude truly *is* everything.

I've studied the topic of humor and everything related to the subject for "umpteen" years. And just when I think there's no way I'd be able to find out anything new about humor — whoops! Some new research comes out disputing previous findings about the issue! Or, lo and behold, someone discovers an answer to controversy and we're having to adjust our way of thinking, speaking and lecturing on the power of humor and its benefits.

Sooooo, for my purpose (that of encouraging people to "lighten up" and not take themselves so seriously), I pretty much eliminate anything in my programs and presentations that requires *brain work*. As a motivational humorist and speaker on the topic of humor and its health benefits, I want my audiences to simply sit back, kick off their shoes, loosen their ties (and anything else they can loosen without getting arrested) and enjoy what I have to share with them.

With the right attitude, even the *sourest* among us *can sweeten up!* And even the most difficult challenges we have to face become a little lighter, when we face them with a smile — and the right perspective!

As I said, I wasn't born knowing this. I learned it the hard way — by surviving some bleak, dark times that helped me realize life is too short to be taken so seriously. This personal realization fuels my interest in the subject of humor as a great healer and underscores my belief that a sense of humor is a vital survival skill.

I read voraciously, attend every seminar or workshop I can find, and I even became a clown as a prerequisite to taking an international trip to spread smiles half a world away. I'm a member of the Applied Association for Therapeutic Humor, past member of the Fellowship of Merry Christians and the Secret Society of Happy People (guess it's not so secret *now!*).

I'm a graduate of the world's largest and oldest clown college, which is sponsored by the University of Wisconsin-LaCrosse Clown Camp.

I'm also Iowa's first Certified Laughter Leader (CLL), earning the moniker in one hilarious weekend workshop with Dr. Steve Wilson, co-founder of the World Laughter Tour, Inc. and a man devoted to spreading the exciting news that laughter is a great way to improve health and well-being.

One of the most valuable lessons I've learned? That you don't necessarily need a reason to laugh to burst out in guffaws! Nope, you can just go ahead and laugh, strictly for the "health" of it!

As the above-mentioned Dr. Wilson says: "No jokes are needed – just let ourselves be silly and laugh for no reason. It's fun in the name of health."

So exactly what is a laughter leader, and what does it mean to be certifiable ... I mean, certified? It means that not only are you in love with laughter and its many benefits, but that you want to share this love with others! All CLLs are encouraged to promote, participate in and foster a love of laughter and get people laughing, even when (or perhaps especially when) they think there's nothing funny to be laughing about, it seems. For more information, contact my friends at www. worldlaughtertour.com.

These experiences, combined with my knowledge of the healthcare field as a registered nurse and personal research, have helped me realize some of the countless benefits of seeking joy every day.

For example, I've learned that laughter can and does:

- Relieve stress.
- Reduce anxiety and tension.
- Boost the immune system.
- Improve and enhance your mood, as it is a natural anti-depressant.
- Reduce physical and emotional pain (bless those little molecules of morphine, better known as endorphins!).
- Improve on-the-job productivity and job satisfaction.
- Lower your blood pressure.
- Lift your self-esteem.
- Boost your mental functioning, making you more alert, creative and improving your memory.
- Benefit your facial, abdominal and chest muscles and other internal organs – a good, hearty belly laugh is especially beneficial.
- I even read somewhere that laughter may even reverse the effects of aging … *hallelujah, there's hope for this old lady yet!*

Laughter has also been known to cause leaking. Not only can a hearty laugh bring you to tears, it can also have you excusing yourself to the nearest rest room, as you find yourself laughing and leaking from both ends!

Research studies prove that when you put a smile on your face, regardless of whether it's a genuine or fake smile (the brain doesn't know the difference), it's utterly impossible to be full of stress and tension. Isn't that neat? What more reason could you need to seek out ways to bring more joy to your life?

Humor can relieve our stress, take our mind off physical symptoms (if even just momentarily) and be an especially helpful technique when working with or caring for people with both physical and mental problems.

I've come to know about the advantages of humor as a great healer not just from reading and attending classes and workshops; I've learned it from my own time in the trenches! I've been in some deep ones, let me tell you. And while I didn't always know to turn to humor as a way out, I do now. And I hope that knowledge helps you when life's rough spots catch up with you.

Two retired professors were vacationing with their wives in the Catskills. As they sat on the veranda, the history professor asked the psychology professor:

"Have you read Marx?"

To which the professor of psychology replied:

"Yes, I think it's these pesky wicker chairs."

> *The trouble with being*
> *punctual is that no one else is*
> *around to appreciate it.*

3
We've All Got to Start Somewhere

When it comes to age, I'm not counting the miles. In fact, I've been turning my odometer back on a daily basis! You want to discuss my Blue Book value? I guess you'd put me in the classic car category — because of my hair color, but not my chassis!

Thankfully, I don't feel my age. I have no idea how *my age* is supposed to feel. I'm too busy enjoying the ride.

Speaking of age reminds me of the time I was scheduled to speak at the Nebraska State Student Nurse Association Conference in Hastings, Neb. My contact person was a young student nurse who found my name through *someone* who obviously had heard me *somewhere* and recommended that she contact me to speak at this conference. So she did. (Trust me — with all the fancy schmancy marketing techniques out there today, I still find word-of-mouth the most successful way to get business.)

This "wet behind the ears" student nurse and I had several lengthy conversations by phone and e-mail to arrange for me to speak at this special event, but we hadn't met face to face.

When I arrived at the conference, I went in to find this young lady to tell her *I had arrived!* Having no idea what she looked like, (nor she me), I stood in the registration area and looking quite "out of place" (that's one way meeting planners can always spot a speaker — he or she is the one person who is standing alone, looking bewildered, weary and confused … which isn't particularly difficult for me).

Soon, a young lady walked toward me and said: "Are you Jenny, our speaker?"

I smiled sweetly and answered "Well, yes, I am."

Then she replied (much too loudly): "Oh my … I didn't realize you were going to be THAT old!"

Keep in mind, this was more than a decade ago, and I wasn't nearly as old THEN as I am today! What did this youngster expect, after all? She was in her early 20s — if even that — EVERYONE was old to her!

This was when I was just getting started in my speaking business; boy, did I have a lot to learn! I became a fast

learner when it came to the use of microphones, all because
of one particular incident ... and that incident also took place
at that very same student nurse conference in Hastings, Neb.
As my time to speak approached, someone brought me a
lavaliere microphone, said "Here's your mike — you're up
next," and turned and walked away.

This was my first experience with a lavaliere microphone,
which consists of a battery pack attached to a *loooooong*
wire that ends with a tiny device that clips to a lapel, collar
or wherever you like — just so it's near your mouth.

Knowing I was soon to be onstage for an extended period, I
did the very last thing a speaker does before performing. You
guessed it — I went to the bathroom! I entered the ladies'
room, hooked my battery pack to the waistband of my skirt,
then proceeded to use the facilities. Several cups of coffee
and my pre-speech glass of water insured I had a full tank,
and I wanted to be on "Empty" when I took the platform.

Having taken care of business, I did the final adjusting,
primping and checking to make sure everything looked good
... including that important last smile to check the teeth for
lipstick/lettuce (oh *come on,* you do that too, and you're not
even a speaker!).

Assuming I was "all systems go," I stood just outside the
open door to the meeting room, carefully listening for my
introduction. Gearing myself up for the talk ahead and getting the butterflies in my stomach to behave, I felt this little
tap on my shoulder. I looked up and there stood a young man
who said in a serious tone: "Ma'am, your MICROPHONE is
ON ... and (dramatic pause) ... it's BEEN on...."

It took a few seconds for his words to sink in and then I realized ... omigosh, I *needed no introduction!* Beyond that threshold sat 125 people who already knew *far more about me than I had ever intended!*

What was I going to do now? How was I going to recover from this private rest room moment turned all-too-public?

I recall my conversation in my head going something like this:

"Okay, Jenny, NOW, what are you going to do? Think, girl, think! Get a grip and get over it! Remember why you're here, after all! To talk to all these future medical profession- als about the power, value and benefits of humor.... So what better time to walk the talk, girl?! Oh, and before you go out there, check your heel for toilet paper...."

It was then that I heard my introduction, which *really* made me sound important (I had written it, after all). I walked in as they were applauding, stopped and faced the audience, all the while thinking of my public visit to the private rest room.

With no sign of a smile whatsoever on my red face, I slowly looked around the room, took a deep breath, tilted my head down and, in an apologetic tone, I reported a simple fact that I knew all of these future healthcare providers could relate to:

"Well. ... Now you know ... (dramatic pause) .... My bodily functions are NORMAL!"

*If you're not making waves,
you're not kicking hard enough!*

4
Should Have Stopped With the First One!

M y life has been interesting ever since it started!

Instead of being born in a hospital, as was becoming the "norm" in those days, I was born at home.

That home was a small house in Watertown, South Dakota where my mother — an unmarried 19-year-old — lived with her mother. The girl was in her second year of nursing school and in love (and apparently showed it once) with a young man who wanted to marry her. She refused, believing that wasn't the way to start a life together and that she needed to finish her schooling. (This was at a time when students in nursing schools were not allowed to be married … let alone have children).

My birth mother made the decision to "give up" her baby, even though her mother encouraged her to keep it. What courage that must have taken! She could have made the safe, "acceptable" choice to marry the boy she loved and start a family. Instead, she made a very difficult choice and, I believe, a courageous one. She believed her child would have more opportunities if she chose adoption. And she made this difficult choice in spite of her mother, who wanted her to keep the baby.

I'd like to think that I inherited my birth mom's grit. I do know that I admire her ability to keep moving forward, even with an unexpected pregnancy. After all, this was a time when pregnancy outside of wedlock was seen as devastatingly shameful.

But my mother didn't sneak off to have an abortion. She didn't go into hiding for fear of shaming the family. She didn't marry a man just to give her baby a father. She chose to carry the baby (me!) to term, deliver me at home and go through with giving me to a loving family.

When her doctor learned of her decision, he told her, "I know a very nice couple who already have a 4-year-old adopted daughter. If you'd like, I could call them to see if they might be interested in adopting your baby, too."

Years later, when I was old enough to understand, my adoptive mother, Caroline, recounted for me the conversation that occurred shortly after I was born:

"Hello, Caroline, this is Dr. Jorgenson. I have just delivered a healthy baby girl who will be needing a loving home, and I was wondering … is there any chance that you and Clarence might like to have another little girl?"

Me, on the left, and my sister, Carol

Here was a life-changing phone call. Not the kind of call where someone asks: "Want to go to lunch?" or "Can I have that recipe for so-and-so" or "Could you *believe* she wore *that* outfit to church?!?!" This call had the power to change the course of history for not just myself, but my birth mother and her family, and my adoptive family — Caroline and Clarence Erickson and their then-only child, Carol.

Still, despite the magnitude of their answer, it took the Ericksons less time than it takes most people to choose pizza toppings to make the decision to bring me into their home.

Again, my mother would tell me later, the conversation continued something like this: "Just a minute, Doctor, while I go ask Clarence…. *Dad, it's Dr. Jorgenson — he wants to know — do we want another baby girl?*" After only a few seconds, she came back with their answer:

"Sure, why not?"

I've often wondered since that day how many times they asked themselves, "Oh, *why* didn't we stop at just one?"

If God is watching,
the least we can do
is be entertaining.

5
Fear of the Lord ... and My Mother!

I believe I had what I consider a normal (is there such a thing?) childhood.

My sister and I had the most loving parents any kids could have. Funny, though, they came from two very different nationalities and backgrounds — our father's ancestry was Norwegian, and our mother was of German heritage. It's a miracle one of them didn't kill the other because of the distinct differences in their makeup.

Dad was soft-spoken, very laid-back, a man of few words, no time for small talk. Matter of fact, now that I take the time to picture him, I don't believe I ever saw my Dad run, skip, hop or even move very fast, let alone hum, sing, or whistle a tune. This was a guy who was SO proper, he would wear a dress hat and tie while mowing the lawn. No kidding!

It wasn't that he was oblivious to the humor around him. He just didn't show any acknowledgement of anything funny. I don't know if he felt it was "against his religion" to let out a great big guffaw every now and again or what.

Dad's stone-faced demeanor did hide a dry wit, I would eventually learn. I distinctly remember in one of the few letters I received from him while I was in nursing school, Dad wrote: "It's been so hot and dry here (South Dakota) that the trees are chasing the dogs around." That was about the extent of my Dad's sense of humor.

Now, Mom was a different story!

This lady knew how to do everything our Dad didn't, or perhaps didn't *want* to do. She was a talker (and how!), a whistler, a singer and occasionally a hummer (not ever in tune). She laughed easily, often and heartily. She loved a good story (clean or unclean) and certainly wasn't above uttering a "four-letter" word if she felt the occasion warranted it!

She was a hard worker, knit or sewed most all of our clothes (not Dad's — his standards must have been a little higher than the rest of ours!), and believed in discipline, *big time!*

We were brought up in the Lutheran faith, and all discipline was enforced by Mom. I'm not sure if Dad just chose not to have anything to say, or if he didn't have the opportunity! Perhaps he was happy with the status quo. Whichever, my mother's lessons stuck. I can't tell you how many times that I told my own kids, "*My* mother would have killed me if I'd done/said this or that." And that was very close to the truth!

My mother was so strict that I used to say, "I have the fear of the Lord AND my mother to worry about!"

You couldn't even give this woman a dirty look without her calling you on it.

For example, when you turned 14 in South Dakota in those days, you were allowed to drive. So I was driving the family car to do errands and occasionally to the state fairgrounds to "hang out" at my beloved horse barns. (I fell in love with horses during a Girl Scout outing to the horse barns at the fairgrounds.)

One afternoon I had just returned from the barns and had gulped down a bottle of soda pop while on the drive home. My family was waiting at the supper table so I ran in, washed up, sat down and up from my belly erupted a massive, unladylike sound that was as unexpected and shocking to me as it was to my family!

I *BELCHED*!

My mom squared her shoulders to look directly at me and said in a very indignant voice, "Well!"

I put a smug look on my face to match hers and said with all the smartaleckness of a teen-ager who has yet to know better: "What'cha expect … chimes?"

I got two weeks without the car.

A little girl had just finished her first week of school. "I'm wasting my time," she said to her mother. "I can't read, I can't write, and they won't let me talk!"

6
School Daze

I stood out in a crowd from an early age.

During school, I was always the second-tallest girl in the class. Come to think of it, I was the second-tallest kid in the whole school! I guess they didn't make tall *boys* in those days.… Consequently, whenever we lined up for class pictures, chorus concerts and the like, I'd always bend my knees just enough to make me the same height as all the rest of the girls … all except for Marilyn, that is.

Marilyn towered over all of us! Meanwhile, I looked as normal as I possibly could for a little while (until my knees began to ache).

Not only did my height set me apart … my mouth did as well. In fact, I was *destined* to be a talker! Just ask my kindergarten teacher. She went through more rolls of adhesive tape that year she had me in class! You see, she seemed to think that putting a piece of tape over my mouth and setting me behind the upright piano would somehow shut me up.

Obviously, all her technique did was give me something to talk about!

Other than the adhesive tape incident, I enjoyed school … especially being with my friends.

In high school, my friends and I were not the girls who dated the "jocks;" we were the girls who dated the nice guys even though they weren't the most popular boys in school. I went steady with a boy a year ahead of me who was half "jock" and half "Average Joe."

He was a nice boy, in every meaning of the term, and knew how to make a girl feel special. I remember him telling my mother, "Some girls smell like girls. Jenny always smells like a horse."

I told you he was a good guy!

I never saw him after high school graduation. I hope he met a nice girl who smelled even *better* than a horse! Although, I can't imagine what that smell would be….

As for me, I had big dreams. Since I already smelled like horses all the time — after all, I *lived* at the horse barns — I decided I was going to Kentucky to train three- and five-gaited horses for rich people. I really felt that was my calling.

Thankfully, my friend and mentor, Dick — a trainer at the horse barns, positive role model in my life and probably my best adult friend since I was 14 — set me straight. He told me simply: "Jenny, I don't think you should do that."

My friend and mentor, Dick the horse trainer, with Skipper

"Why not? You taught me so much and I think I can do it."

"I need to tell you that you'll never be accepted. You go down South, you're always going to be a Yankee girl, and you'll never be anything but."

I didn't argue with him. I trusted him. This kind-hearted, gray-haired, horse-loving man, older than dirt, obviously knew more about the world in the 1950s than I did.

So I changed my career path.

Luckily, my best friend Mert had already decided she wanted to be a nurse. So I hitched my wagon to hers, and off we went, to take the nursing world by storm!

Show up early and stay late. (You learn the best secrets that way!)

7
Three Tough Years

When I think of my three years of nurse's training, I'm reminded of the long hours, the hard work, and of being scared to death most of the time.

Would you believe I never missed a day of nurse's training? Was it conscientiousness on my part? No, it was fear. I was scared to death I'd miss something. So I always showed up. Even on days I was sicker than the patient I was taking care of, I showed up. Still, it was hard for me to not grab a corner of her hospital blanket and say: "Move over and let me in!"

We had only 30 minutes of free time every evening on weeknights and not much more on weekends. Those were difficult years; years where I made my own fun because if I hadn't, there wouldn't have been any. Sure, when you get a bunch of 18- and 19-year-old girls together, there's going to be lots of giggling and horsin' around. Ex-Lax in the fudge? Short-sheeted beds? Peanut butter toast at 4 in the morning? Pooling our pennies to buy a brownie at the corner bakery to share? You don't think *your* generation invented those coping techniques, do you?

My roommate Mert and I had grown up together and knew each other like sisters. This was our first time away from home, and we had our share of homesickness. I'm not sure if I would have made it through those years without the support and love of my dear friend. We shared the fun and the struggles together and somehow survived!

The most long-standing lesson I learned in those three years had nothing to do with IVs, enemas or how to carry a bedpan without spilling it on your white shoes. I learned the all-important lesson of finding humor wherever you could.

For instance, I developed a talent for finding the "funny" in stressful situations and quickly learned that humor could help defuse even the most difficult instances. It's been said that humor can be a coping tool, and that's exactly what it was to me, time and time again.

Have you ever been SO exhausted you thought *everything* was funny? And you laughed so hard you couldn't stop ... your cheeks hurt and your muscles in your legs became so weak you had to sit down?

I remember one night as a student, working the graveyard shift with another student whom I'll call Ellen. In those days, they put us in charge of an entire floor!

We were having a very busy night, running from patient to patient and room to room. Meds here, bedpans there. The stress kept building and building and building … until *something* had to give.

And that *something* was me.

For one brief moment, Ellen and I found ourselves in the nurse's station at the same time. I don't recall who said what, but I do recall it struck us directly in our funny bones. We burst out laughing, and I couldn't stop.

I buckled over and actually had to lie down on the floor in the middle of the nurse's station as I rolled around in convulsive laughter. When I finally recovered and lay there catching my breath, I recall that I felt much more than just plain happy. I actually felt euphoric. It was such a peaceful, relaxing feeling that I hated to have to get up and have it end.

I had experienced a "high" without any drugs!

That's powerful stuff.

Even though that night took place more than 50 years ago, I remember it like it was yesterday. I hope that everyone has that same experience of a natural high at least once in his or her life. And never think that everything you learn in school you read in the text books!

> *"Laughter is the shortest distance between two people."*
> — Victor Borge

8

A Good Trade

As an 18-year-old student nurse, born and raised in a small South Dakota town, I found myself facing new — and often intimidating — experiences every day. It was 1953, and I was working in a small general hospital in Sioux City, Iowa, learning my trade.

This particular day, I faced a number of "firsts" all wrapped up in the same patient.

This was my first time in the eight-bed men's ward, the first time caring for a male patient close to my own age, and the first time caring for a person of a different race than myself. (This is no biggie nowadays, but keep in mind that the time was the 1950s, the setting was Iowa, and the student nurse involved — *me* — was intimidated to even *be* in the men's ward, not to mention feeling quite inadequate when it came to providing *real, live patients* with *actual clinical care*).

This was when hospitals had separate men's and women's wards with several beds in a single large room. The only way to provide any patient privacy was to wheel a screen between the beds. I had to garner up a lot of courage to give this man the care he needed while also appearing competent and professional — when I was feeling anything but! This young man was on complete bed rest requiring total care. And here he was, poor fellow, assigned ME to provide that care!

Thankfully, my nurse's training kicked in, and, rather hesitantly, I approached him and introduced myself. "Good morning, my name is Jenny, and I'm here to give you your bed bath."

My patient's face showed some of the same emotions I was feeling — "Oh, *this IS* going to be awkward!"

We were both uncomfortable. Luckily, I'm a nervous talker. When I get nervous, boy can I talk! So I started asking questions.... "Where you from?" ... "Any brothers and sisters?" ... "Are you still in school?" ... and on I rambled.

His answers came stutteringly at first, but soon, we were chatting comfortably, even laughing (although much of it was nervous laughter), but the laughter broke the ice and boy, did it help break down barriers. The awkwardness was starting to disappear and a bonding was taking place.

When I had finished my tasks — feeling much more competent and at ease, I might add — I asked that all-important

question: "Is there any-
thing else I can do
for you before I leave?"
He looked around the
stark surroundings —
plain walls, white beds,
white privacy screens on
wheels, steel gray equip-
ment — then looked at
me and said: "Is there
any way you could get
me a magazine or some-
thing to help pass the
time away?"

*Graduation, Lutheran
School of Nursing 1955*

His question put me into his shoes for just a moment — the
shoes of a young man, frightened for his health, far from
loved ones, alone in a strange environment with nothing
much to do and nobody to do it with.

I, too, was far from loved ones, but had many new friends to
help me spend what little free time I had. To keep me company when I studied, I had a smart little alarm clock/radio
— a going-away gift from my parents when I left for nursing
school, and a much-treasured possession.

I got an idea.

"You think you might like to listen to the radio?" I asked.

He said he sure would, but didn't own one. And with no family or friends in town, he couldn't think of anyone to call to
bring a radio, a book or anything else.

So I told my new friend I'd be back with a surprise. I noted a spark of anxiety in his eyes when I said the word "surprise!"

I went to my dormitory room and tucked the cherished radio under my coat. I headed back to the hospital, ran up the steps and into the men's ward. With two hands, I held out the radio to my patient and said, "Here! Why don't you borrow my radio while you're here?"

The smile on his face — probably half joy from seeing the radio and half relief in realizing the "surprise" I had promised had nothing to do with a needle or bed pan — was heartwarming. I can still see him grinning from ear to ear, his eyes sparkling with joy.

I cleared a spot on his bedside table for the little radio, plugged it in and showed him how to tune in local stations. Then I said goodbye, telling him I'd stop in and see him as often as I could and pick up the radio when he was dismissed.

Several days went by and I got busy with my class schedule and work assignments. Finally, when I found time to get back to the men's ward, I walked up to the bed my friend had occupied, peeked around the curtain … and saw a stripped, empty bed. The bedside table was cleared off, too — except for my radio.

My radio — in three pieces.

My heart sunk in my chest — my prized possession, gone! I slowly, unbelievingly, walked up to the bedside table. Disappointment flooded over me. The lump in my throat grew bigger with each step. I thought I might even cry….

Then I saw a half-sheet of paper tucked under the radio. Written in sharp, staccato pencil was a brief note:

> Dear Nurse Jenny,
> Sorry about your radio. It fell on the floor and broke. Thanks for letting me use it. You are a good nurse.
> Jim

I was sad to see my radio in pieces. But the tears that came after reading the note weren't because of what I had lost. They were for what I had learned: In nursing, it sometimes takes a bit of sacrifice to bring a smile to a patient's face.

And that smile is worth more than just about anything.

Two elderly gentlemen from a retirement center were sitting on a bench under a tree when one turns to the other and says: "Slim, I'm 83 years old now and I'm just full of aches and pains. I know you're about my age. How do you feel?"

Slim says, "I feel just like a newborn baby."

"Really!? Like a newborn baby!?"

"Yep. No hair, no teeth, and I think I just wet my pants."

*Why didn't Noah swat
those two mosquitoes?*

9
A Whistle and a Prayer

While I may have discovered the healing power of humor in nursing school, I wouldn't realize its true strength until a few years later, when life tossed me a major curve ball that I somehow managed to survive.

And it all started when, as an almost-graduated nursing student, I was hanging out with some friends on the steps of the house where we roomed.

As we perched and posed outside the mansion that housed our rooms (and, just in case you're interested, would one day become the Sioux City Public Museum), some strapping young men drove by and whistled at us.

We whistled back.

They came back around the block and introduced themselves. The tallest one — the guy with the grin that didn't
stop — was named Frank Martin.

Frank had just been discharged from the army that very
week, and we hit it off almost immediately! And in the sum-
mer of 1956, I became Mrs. Frank Martin.

Mrs. Frank Martin.... I thought I'd go to my grave with that
name, but that was not to be.

Frank with our first son, Kirk

Our boys, Eric, left, and Kirk

"All things work together for good to them that love the Lord, to those that are called according to His purpose."

Romans: 8:28

10
One Last Kiss

I firmly believe that a sense of humor is not only nice to have, it's profoundly vital if you're going to do more than just survive in this world. I also know that a firm belief in God and a strong sense of humor are two keys to survival. As Bill Cosby says, "If you can laugh at it, you can survive it."

And goodness knows, I'm a survivor.

The scene: A little white tract house in Norfolk, Nebraska, where I live with my husband, Frank, our two sons, Kirk (2 1/2 years old) and Eric (12 months). We're both 27 years old, he a heating/air conditioning technician, me a nurse working the 3-to-11 shift at a local hospital, both so busy with our jobs and children and loving every minute of it. At 8 o'clock the morning of July 19, 1960, I kiss Frank's freshly shaved face goodbye as he leaves for work. It's my day off from my nursing job so I'm busy all day with my usual household chores and tending to the boys.

A typical start to a day that would forever alter my life and the lives of my sons.

Just a few minutes after 5 p.m. the phone rings. It's a nurse at the Lutheran Community Hospital where I work telling me that Frank has been in an accident.

A very serious accident.

"Come as quickly as you can, Jenny," the nurse says, her tone telling me that this is very serious. I call a neighbor to come stay with my boys and another to drive me to the hospital.

I enter the familiar hospital where I work, see the faces of people I see every day, and am led to the operating room where I see the face of my love.

Frank is lying unconscious, his brain hemorrhaging from a basal skull fracture caused when a commercial freezer he was filling with refrigerant gas exploded, knocking him backward onto the concrete floor.

I see it on their faces before I even talk to them – the nurses and doctors are helpless, unable to stop the bleeding.

Someone pulls up a stool and says in that pity-filled tone of voice you hate to hear because it makes you realize just how helpless everyone around you is: "You're welcome to sit here with him...."

I perch on the stool and look down at the face I had quickly kissed goodbye that morning, the face that had lit up with pride both times the doctors had told him, "It's a boy!" .... The face that was the last thing I saw each night and the first thing I saw each morning. The face I thought I would see beside me for a lifetime.

The tears run down my cheeks. I feel the comforting hands on my shoulders and the soft words of everyone around me — doctors, fellow nurses, my pastor — and I sense something ... Someone ... greater than all is there beside me as well. I am aware that the Lord is with me, too. I can feel His strength, and because He is with me, I don't fall apart.

The doctors and nurses make it clear that there's nothing they can do. And so I realize that my husband and I are both in His hands.

I'm there when my husband of five short years, the father of my two beautiful boys, takes his last breath.

I kiss his face goodbye for the last time. The nurses and pastor lead me out of the room. Someone gives me a tranquilizer, and I am sent home.

He who laughs, lasts.

11
Saying Goodbye and Looking Ahead

The whole town turned out for Frank's funeral.

Everyone knew him because of his job and his friendly nature. And everyone wanted to let me know how much he would be missed. I am still amazed when I think of the flowers and sympathy and consideration the folks in that little town shared with me and my boys.

Ironically, a friend of ours, Chuck, had just opened a mortuary, so of course he was the one to handle the funeral arrangements. To this day, I wonder how difficult it was for him to take care of the preparations for his dear friend….

Since I buried Frank at Memorial Park Cemetery in Sioux City, Iowa (where my parents were then living), we had a funeral procession the entire 81 miles from Norfolk to Sioux City. That was the longest, quietest 81 miles I have ever traveled. Reality hadn't set in for me yet; I had left the boys with friends in Norfolk, so I had nothing to do but sit and think.

And all I could think was: "This can't be happening to me."

When I look back at that time today, I realize now that the Lord sustained me through this heart-wrenching, heart-breaking time.

What can your friends and family do but give you a hug, cry with you, hold your hand, bring over a hot dish? The one whose hands you really have to put your whole life in is the Lord. That's what I've done. That's what I did then, and that's what I continue to do, each and every day.

Frank's death left me so unprepared in so many ways. My most difficult challenge was telling Kirk that Daddy was gone. How do you tell a 2 ½ year old that he'll never see his Daddy again?

Those were the times I needed the strength of God that I had felt so strongly in the operating room. And I inevitably found that strength, along with the courage to move forward.

While Eric, the baby, was too young to understand that his dad wasn't coming back, Kirk knew something was different. He and Frank had been very close, and the death of his big, happy-go-lucky father left a huge void in the little fellow's life.

Frank loved children — not just his own — he loved all kids. At 6-foot-4, Frank was, as my dad said, "one tall drink of water." He came from a family of 10 kids.

When you entered the home of Frank's parents, you were surrounded by boisterous laughter and love. Money was so tight that their mother, Rose, would sew buttons on the inside knees of their blue jeans so the boys wouldn't get down on their knees and wear holes in the fabric.

For a treat, they'd have a bowl of popcorn topped with milk and a little sugar.

The Martin home was pretty much the exact opposite of the tightly run, two-child ship I had been raised in, and it was a bit of a culture shock for me.

Sunday afternoons with Frank's family meant fried chicken and "smashed" potatoes with as many as 30 people for dinner. The older you were, the better chance you had for sitting at the table; the younger you were, the more likely you would be to park your plate upon a newspaper place mat on the floor that surrounded the huge table.

All this was commonplace to the Martins but absolutely foreign to me.

While the Martins were a warm, loving family, they weren't much of a church-going family. Frank had been baptized in the Salvation Army church, so he was a child of God, and for that I was grateful. At his funeral, his family was overcome with anger and grief and questions of how and why such a tragedy could happen.

As I witnessed their anger and frustration, I silently thanked my parents for raising me as a Christian with an understanding of the hereafter and knowledge that Frank and I will be together again some day. All my strength on that day and from that day on comes from Him. Sure, I don't know why Frank was taken from us, but I feel there is a reason for everything that happens.

In my case, I have come to realize that Frank's death gave me the resolve and determination to become the best mother that I could possibly be.

You Never Know
(Author Unknown)

You never know when someone
Might catch a dream from you.
Or something you say
May open up the windows
Of a mind that seeks light;
The way you live
May not matter at all,
But you never know, it might.

And just in case it could be
That another's life, through you,
Might possibly change for the better
With a better and brighter view,
It seems it might be worth a try
At pointing the way to the right;
Of course, it may not matter at all,
But then again, it might.

*Hospitality: Making your
guests feel at home, even if
you wish they were.*

12
Returning to the Nest

When I called my mother to tell her what had happened to Frank, I remember saying over and over again: "What'll I do, Mom? What'll I do?"

And my mother, the wise woman she was, simply said, without a moment's hesitation in a calm, anchoring voice: "Jenny, you'll come home and live with us."

So, within seven days of becoming a widow at age 27, I had quit my job; sold, given away or stored what few possessions we had owned and told my dear friends and neighbors goodbye. I loaded up my 1953 Chevrolet sedan and my boys and headed northeast. We traveled along the same route I had taken by myself just a few days earlier to bury Frank.

42 / You Laugh, I'll Drive

The three of us began a new chapter of our lives.

So here we were, my parents, myself and my sons, in a tiny two-bedroom bungalow in Sioux City, Iowa. I honestly don't remember doing much laughing back then. I do remember having a supportive family, the love of my two little boys, and the strength of my Savior. That's what sustained me.

Not that I didn't have tough times. I had a lot of them. There were days it took all my strength to put both feet on the floor and pull myself out of bed. Nights of intense loneliness. The stress and chaos and fear of wondering what the future would hold. But I got through it, day by day, turning to the things that brought me peace and joy — my family, and most of all, my children.

I was so young. I didn't understand the sacrifice my parents must have made. Can you imagine? They had given up their larger bedroom to make room for a crib and a double bed for myself and my two boys. My parents moved into the smaller room that my mother had recently made into a sitting/sewing room. So much for sitting and sewing!

Sacrificing their peace and quiet and routine and privacy must have been very, very hard; yet I never heard my Mom or my Dad complain. Not once. They were nothing but supportive. And it's not because we didn't give them reason to complain! A weepy, widowed young woman and two rambunctious boys under the age of 3 would make Mother Teresa say, "God, help me!"

I know today that the Lord was watching over my parents, too, giving them the strength and patience needed to carry their daughter and grandsons through this challenging time.

Not that patience and hard work and sacrifice were new to my parents.

My dad was a railway mail clerk. He would leave very early in the morning, get on the train and travel up to 300 miles, standing sorting mail *aaaaallll* the way there and *aaaallll* the way back. Have you ever tried standing on a moving train? Now think about doing it … standing, swaying, jolting, all the while sorting mail, for hour upon hour, mile upon mile.

And he did this for 42 years.

My mother was a housewife, proudly taking care of hearth and home.

So imagine the changes we brought — the noises and messes that two little boys can make; the tears they had to put up with from me; my brief periods of depression, crying spells at the drop of a hat (I admit I had the "woe is me" attitude).

And yet my mother's wisdom continued to direct me. I can remember distinctly the day she turned to me and said: "Jenny. You're not the first woman to lose her husband. And you're not going to be the last."

That seemed so cruel at the time. How could she say that to me? But today those words don't come back to haunt me; they come back to help me understand what she was trying to say: "Buck up, girl. Deal with it and move on."

In the years that followed, people would often tell me what a wonderful job I did with my boys. And I'd tell them, "Thank you. I never could have done it without the help of my mother and the Lord."

My mom was right there, holding my feet to the fire to be a good parent. She was a great backup — mostly because she was always on my back!

She was such a good role model. I can remember time after time, I would tell my kids to quit doing something, and they wouldn't quit. (After all, they were normal kids.) So then it would take my mother to say, "Jenny, I believe you've told them to stop it. Once you've told them something, you need to follow through." And that has stuck with me all my life.

But on the day she told me that I wasn't the first woman to lose her husband, and I wouldn't be the last, she reminded me that my challenges in life were not unique. That day, I realized I had to look ahead and move ahead.

Besides my broken heart, Frank had left me $42,000 in life insurance. That was quite a bit in 1960. So my parents and I started talking about my getting a place of my own. (Patience or not, I'm sure that as the months wore on, our welcome was wearing a little thin. After all, they say that house guests, like fish, start to stink after three days. We'd been there for nine months, and boy, we must have really reeked!)

My mom knew a builder, I picked out my lot and chose a modular home. In March of 1961, my sons and I moved into our very own paid-for little bungalow on Cypress Street. That was a real milestone in my life — owning this two-bedroom home with the unfinished basement, attached garage, bare essentials, for a whopping $13,500, which I paid the moment we walked in the door.

Of course, even that milestone didn't come without a lesson. I naively paid for the house with cash. Some shady dealings by the builder nearly prevented me from getting the deed to my home. That was scary, very scary. If not for the work of a good lawyer, the boys and I would have been back in my parents' home and $13,500 poorer.

Fortunately, the deed came through and, while I've changed many things in my life in the 45 years since, one thing that I haven't changed is my address: I still live in my little house to this day.

As a 5-year-old boy and his mother were headed to McDonald's one day, they passed a car accident.

Thinking of the people involved, the mother told her son: "We should say a prayer."

Obviously thinking more about his stomach, the little boy put his hands together and said earnestly:

"Please, God, don't let those cars block the entrance to McDonald's."

*My dad with his
grandsons*

Eric, 17 months, and Kirk, 3, at
Grandma and Grandpa's

*My mother with her grandsons
Kirk, left, and Eric*

*Honk if you love
peace and quiet!*

13
Little House on Cypress Street

I felt like a pioneer lady.

Ours was the only house on the west side of Cypress Street.
My back yard was nothing but cornfields. Talk about a
typical Iowa homestead scenario! But in this case, the corn
wasn't mine. I didn't have to worry about it. I had my own
crop in the front yard — my own crop of mud, that is.

No sidewalk, no street, just a big gully where they put pipes
that would one day connect to the neighbors' houses, when
they were built. Meanwhile, I had a house sitting on a piece
of land where there was nothing.

For me and my boys, it was *everything!*

I can still see my younger son playing in the ditch in his diaper. I remember walking on planks down to the end of the block, where I had to park my car because in the rainy season the road was pure mud. Kirk wanted to walk in the mud — you try to keep a young boy on the planks when there's squishy mud all around!

As houses started popping up around us, the hardest part of being alone with two little boys was the time between 5:30 and 6 o'clock weeknights. This was the time dads were coming home from work. The boys would watch the other dads come home and the fact that their dad was *not* coming home would be fresh in our minds once more.

I even lamented over the fact that my boys would never get into a shouting match with other boys, that they'd never have the chance to say: "My dad is stronger/bigger/smarter than your dad!"

I realized that being the best mom I could be meant doing the Dad thing, too. Thank God I had been a tomboy! I loved tennis and softball and nearly all those things boys loved to do.

I taught my boys how to throw and catch a baseball. I taught Kirk until he got good enough and strong enough and old enough so that when he would throw to me, I would end up with black-and-blue fingers. I knew it was time to quit when his pitches left blood blisters in the palm of my baseball-gloved hand. He went on without my tutelage to be a pretty good baseball player in his youth! My little guy, Eric, went on to become a powerful little catcher.

I never missed a Little League, Youth League or other game in which either boy played. And nobody had any trouble knowing who *their* mother was. Could it be because I was the loudest, most boisterous parent in the bleachers?

It was all "way to go kid! Come on boys! That's my boy!" All positive, encouraging, "proud Mom" stuff! That's what I'd call it anyway! My boys may have another description. They were probably turning their eyes the other way and swearing under their breath, "Oh gawwwd, there's *my mom*."

Still, it was important to me that my kids knew I was *always* there. They could always count on me. And while I may have been sitting (or standing, or jumping) on the sidelines, my heart was right down on that field. Throwing every ball. Running every base. Judging every pitch. I didn't go to just *watch* the game, I *lived* it!

I made up for two parents ... and THEN SOME!

Some people probably went to the games for fellowship or the gossip or the fresh air or the sunburns. I went because that was *my* boy out there!

The sad part, when Kirk — who was tall and lanky (the spittin' image of his dad) and probably could be a star basketball player — was old enough to start helping with the family income, I made him quit sports to start working. I still have some guilt out of that (what good mother doesn't have some guilt for one choice or another she could have made differently?), but I was a widowed mom with two growing boys, and we were living off Social Security.

I entered both my sons in our local "Rent-a-Kid" program at age 14. No loafing time for them! The boys helped install window air conditioners and did odd jobs. You talk about odd jobs, they did it! They got paid little or nothing, but this was *their* money. It allowed them spending money to buy an 8-track or cassette, go to the movies, pick up a burger now and then and do all those all-important "guy things" that teen-age boys do.

When my boys turned 16, they began "official" jobs after school and weekends. Again, you name it, they probably did it — working in filling stations pumping gas and cleaning windshields; in bowling alleys setting up pins; delivering pizzas, and then working at department stores. After high school graduation, they enrolled in the auto mechanic classes at Western Iowa Technical Community College in Sioux City, which gave them the solid background for their careers.

They went on to work for trucking firms as mechanics. Now, Kirk is a sales representative for Wilson Trailer Co. based in Sioux City; Eric is an executive vice president of Peterson Power Co., California's largest Caterpillar dealership.

But most importantly, they're good people with great senses of humor! And they still manage to make it home to visit every now and then — after all, it's not like they couldn't find the place!

A little boy called his grandmother to wish her a happy birthday. When he asked her how old she was, she told him frankly: "Well, I'm 62 today!" After a moment of silence, the little boy asked: "Did you start at 1?"

Me, my boys and "Tiny" in the little house on Cypress Street

Eric, ace catcher, and Kirk, pitcher extraordinaire!

> *The tail is a dog's*
> *PR department.*

14
When All Else Fails, Get a Puppy!

As a single parent who had suffered such a devastating loss, I had a lingering fear: "What if something like this happens again? *What if something happens to my boys?*"

I imagined all kinds of harm coming to my children. I know every mother goes through that, but probably not as intensely as I did. So I decided I needed a security system.

The fancy, high-tech security system I chose? A 12-pound, 3-month-old boxer puppy we named "Tiny."

Some security.

Ever been around a boxer puppy?

They're the most lovable, bumbling, clumsy, big-footed masses of canine energy you'll ever see! The only thing Tiny "watched out for" was something anyone might put in his or her mouth, just in case he could catch a loose crumb before it hit the linoleum. This dog loved everybody! And while he may not have had the attitude to be a guard dog, he had the looks of one.

I didn't worry much about anyone harming my boys or breaking in, because the first thing anyone approaching our home would see was this big black muzzle and mouth full of teeth. They didn't know those teeth never sunk into anything more dangerous than a squeaky toy. They also had no idea that the remaining 90 percent of Tiny was doing the "happy doggy wiggle" in anticipation of meeting a new friend!

Tiny loved life in the little house on Cypress Street and, more importantly, with two boys for his playmates! He eradicated every garter snake in our yard with so much gusto that I think half of those snakes died of sheer fright! Even Kirk's painted turtle met its fate in the backyard after somebody forgot it was out there and somebody else let Tiny out. I think this turtle succumbed to combat fatigue from being tossed, pawed, rolled on, chewed up and spit out ... because Tiny felt it wasn't cooperating and ceased to be fun anymore.

Nothing was safe in that backyard, and yet there wasn't a mean bone in that dog's body. All that dog knew was play.

Still, I realized that Tiny needed a little more direction than he was getting from the boys. So I looked into obedience training through the Sioux Valley Kennel Club, and took my first step toward what would become a lifelong passion: Training and showing dogs.

Tiny didn't go on to win any ribbons, however; he had a little too much "boy" in him to make the cut. OK, let me be a bit more specific: He flunked.

No one from the obedience school officially issued a report card with a big "F" on it, but I guess "flunking" is what you call it when you say, "Tiny, COME!" and he's busy working the room, wiggling his heart into everyone around him.

But I wasn't going to let one failure, in the form of a 50-pound nonstop wagging machine, get the best of me. So I decided to take on a much more formidable partner — a 5-pound, smoky-black toy poodle named Tina.

Tiny the boxer and Tina the toy poodle got along famously. They would play and play, with the boys running right along with them. And when the moose that was Tiny finally laid down after a busy day with the boys, he'd lay on his side with his big ear flopped out. Within minutes, along would come petite Tina, and she'd curl up in that silky ear flap.

The two would nap the hours away, content and unconditionally loving one another.

From then on, many dogs entered my life and, as they say, left their paw prints forever on my heart.

My very first real, official "show dog" I purchased from a breeder friend in Denton, Texas. The dog's name was Whimsy, and she was a jet-black, blue-blooded miniature poodle from a long line of award-winning canines.

I told the breeder/friend that I knew nothing about grooming, training or anything else it would take to turn the little ball of fur into a champion. But, from her phone line in Texas to mine in Iowa, she sold Whimsy with the promise:

"Jenny, don't worry. I'm sending you a puppy that will *show herself*." And boy, did she!

I bought her sight unseen with total ignorance on what to do to make her a champion, and I knew from the minute she strutted out of her kennel-aire at that airport, she had potential *galore!*

I am so grateful to my Texas friend and everyone else whose brains I picked to learn how to show this dog. With their help, and my tenacity, Whimsy — owner-trained, owner-handled and owner-groomed — strutted to her American Kennel Club Championship at just 2 years of age. She earned her Canadian Championship and earned rank as one of the top 50 miniature poodles in the United States for three years running. To put the frosting on the cake (or the gravy on the biscuit?) she earned her companion dog/obedience degree, all while in show coat.

Big goals? I had 'em. And Whimsy helped me reach them.

Through all the hard work, travel, long hours and patience on both of our parts, Whimsy became my best friend. But come to think of it, all my dogs have been my best friends.

I eventually bred my beloved Whimsy with hopes of starting all over with her daughter and achieving greatness once again. I picked out the best mate I could find and Whimsy had four puppies — three males and my much-hoped-for female. Sadly, the tiny female was too frail to survive. She died a day after birth.

I had experienced the joy of working with dogs. Now I had experienced the heartbreak.

Still, do you need a sense of humor to show dogs? It's not a requirement, but it sure helps. (Have you SEEN some of those hairdos on those four-legged creatures?) But I wasn't working on my sense of humor when I began showing dogs. I was stretching my self-confidence muscles and gaining a self-assurance that continues to buoy me today.

It takes guts to show and work with dogs. And if I didn't have any when I started to show dogs, I sure had plenty after 30 years of doing so.

My pets became my therapy. Where some people in my situation may have turned to drink (I considered that, but am not fond of the taste of alcohol), others to gambling or food, I turned to lots and lots of hard work with my animals.

To this day, I swear by pet therapy of ANY kind! In fact, my newest best friend is Roxy, a Toy Fox Terrier. She and I are working hard toward her certification as an international pet therapy dog and, in our spare time, put on an obedience degree or two.

Sign on a small-town animal control office:
The license fee for altered dogs with a certificate
will be $3 and for pets owned by senior citizens
who have not been altered the fee will be $1.50.

*Tiny and Tina —
inseparable pals!*

*Me with my
award-winning Whimsy*

Does the name Pavlov
ring a bell?

15
Head 'Em Up, Move 'Em Out, Rawhide!

Luckily, as I mentioned, my tom-boy upbringing carried me a long way with my sons. Not only did I share my love of dogs with them, I also shared my love of horses.

My love of all things equine began on a Girl Scout outing to a horse barn. It was here that I met the afore-mentioned Dick, a grandfatherly type whom I figured knew more about horses than just about anyone. I was 13 years old and thought Dick was the most fascinating person I had met. During that outing, I probably asked him more questions than he's ever been asked!

After the outing, I couldn't stop thinking about the horses. I loved the way they looked. I loved the way they smelled. I loved the way they nickered when I brushed them. I loved the freedom I felt while riding them.

To this day, I love the smell of horses.... Don't you?

I wanted to go back. I had to go back.

So I did. Every chance I could get, I had my mom or dad or somebody take me out to the horse barns until I was old enough to drive there myself. I spent every Saturday and Sunday I could "hanging out" at the horse barns.

I knew I had learned my horsemanship skills — and apparently Dick's trust — the day he let me ride his horse, Skipper. From then on, he asked and received permission from some of the other owners to have me exercise their horses.

Talk about a dream gig!

This may have been my first unpaid job which I loved, but it wouldn't be the last. In my senior year in high school, I bought an orphan colt for $12 that Dick let me board at the barns in exchange for my helping with the chores.

I named my prize Diablo, and since he was too young to ride, he followed me around on my chores like a puppy. I told him my secrets and he kept them. I went to sleep and woke up thinking of him, and went to see him nearly every day after school and on the weekends.

But life moves ahead, and sometimes our dreams get left alongside the road … at least for a little while.

My beloved Diablo

I had graduated from high school and was going out of town to nursing school and wouldn't be able to take care of Diablo. I had to sell him. Telling Diablo goodbye was one of the saddest days of my young life.

When I left Diablo behind for my education and career, I figured my horse-riding days were over. But sometimes, having children reminds you of the things you loved about your own childhood, and leads you back to those things.

On the outskirts of Sioux City just a few miles from our little house was a riding stable, the Flying W, owned by Mike and Lois Wilson. I would take my boys, then 9 and 7, to watch the horses. Soon, the Wilsons became our very good friends. We began joining in trail rides and building a circle of friends whose lives revolved around their love of horses. I felt it was time to own a horse again.

If there's one "advantage" to being widowed, it is knowing that you can make decisions based solely on your own preferences! So I went to a horse sale with the intention of buying *just one* horse … how was I to know it would be a clearance sale? I ended up buying three!

I'd love to tell you that the three horses were the most well-behaved, warm, wonderful creatures, and that with them, my boys and I spent countless hours exploring the Iowa hillside.

But then I'd be lying.

*Blessed are they who can laugh
at themselves for they shall
never cease to be amused.*

16
Went In for a Horse,
Came Out With a Husband

Here I was at my first horse auction ever, and I couldn't stop raising my hand!

The excitement and chaos of the auction and my love of horses got the best of me. I just kept raising my hand! I wound up with one unbroken stallion colt, one so-so palomino and a third horse I can't even recall — so it must not have left much of an impression on anything but my pocketbook!

What was I thinking? Obviously, I WASN'T! I had two little boys to raise — what was I going to do with three horses? Thankfully, I got that beloved horse smell out of my nostrils long enough to clear my head. I sold the horses over the next few days, and there I was, after my first and last horse auction ever, horseless … but a whole lot wiser.

A few months later, an acquaintance told me about a sweet bay mare named Shy, perfect for me and the boys. With Shy, I began to ride horseback regularly with the Wilsons and other folks who boarded their horses at their stable.

In my circle of "horse people" was a certain handsome older gentleman named Dwight Herrick. He and I became good friends, but that's as far as the relationship went then, since he was married and I wasn't looking to be.

Three years later, when Dwight was divorced and I was teaching dog training, he called me to help train his dachshund. Our friendship sparked into romance, and we soon married (Dwight and me, not the dachshund and me).

We were all so excited! My boys, excited with the possibility of having a father figure in their life. Me, enthralled with this handsome man who shared some of my passions and who couldn't have been nicer to my beloved boys. We loved him! We were more than ready to add him to our family and start living The American Dream!

Unfortunately, within our first year of marriage, Dwight's true colors came out. And they weren't red, white and blue.

He wasn't the compassionate, loving father figure as I had seen before the vows. I had truly believed he would be perfect for me and my sons. But here he was, disciplining my sons harshly and for almost no reason, driving a wedge between the boys and me, trying to break our tight-knit bond.

True, my boys and I were three peas in a pod, and it's hard to squeeze yourself in between something like that. Dwight tried to discipline my boys. I stood up to him. My boys — due to their love and respect for me, I believe — kept their mouths shut as their step dad tried to run our household according to his harsh standards.

I couldn't find the courage or strength or the whatever-it-was to get myself and my boys out of the situation, so the three of us just tolerated it.

Trying to keep the peace and spare my boys from Dwight's harsh words had me constantly on guard and constantly worried. I was caught in the middle. I had knots in my stomach and pains in my chest. I had a headache 24/7. Worst of all, I put on an act like you wouldn't believe for my friends, my family — and, probably most sadly, myself — to give the impression we were the dream family rather than the nightmare we had actually become.

These were the darkest years of my life.

And then … the light at the end of the tunnel … and it wasn't an oncoming train! I became pregnant!

With the birth of our daughter, Jana, Dwight became a proud new papa at age 55, and I was amazed to have become a mother again at 39. What a blessing!

For a brief period, life was not so dark, at least not for my boys. The focus was on our new baby, and the boys had a reprieve from Dwight's controlling ways. For me, however, the tension only increased. I lived in fear of the boys waking the baby and lighting the fire under Dwight once more.

*Love may be blind, but
marriage is a real eye-opener!*

17
It's Now or Never

When Jana was about 3 years old and the boys, 16 and 18, I told Dwight we couldn't go on living under the same roof. I had *had* it.

Even though we both loved Jana, I could no longer tolerate his behavior. I was living a lie — pretending to the world that all was wonderful, admitting only to my parents and two close friends the painful truth – and was plain tired of it.

Finally, my survival instincts overtook my pride. I was ready to begin clawing my way back up to a better life — without Dwight to drag me back down. A part of me knew that it was now or never to make this courageous change. I chose *now*, and told him to get out of my little house on Cypress Street.

I filed for divorce, but when it came time for Dwight to sign the papers, he came up with what he considered "a better plan:" For us to stay married but live under separate roofs. So while we maintained our married status until Dwight's death in 2001, we lived apart since 1975.

We got along much better those 26 years we lived apart; in many ways, it was like we were dating again. We vacationed, celebrated holidays, enjoyed meals and attended church together. We did everything married couples did. He stayed fully involved in Jana's life. When I began my speaking business, he enjoyed driving me to the sites and attending my programs. I'd like to think he tagged along to hear me speak; but I know the promise of a free meal didn't hurt!

Still, I knew Dwight was proud to be seen with me, and it was important for me that we maintained a civil relationship, for our daughter's sake. And to his dying day, we were a couple, Mr. and Mrs. Herrick, who simply chose to keep our separate living arrangements private.

And while he didn't prove to be the piece that would make our little family complete, Dwight did give me a precious gift: My daughter.

Dwight and me, partnering up on a volunteer project ... and a Honda!

> *Time may be a great healer,*
> *but it's a lousy beautician.*

18
Sons are Sons 'til They Take a Wife, But Daughters Stick Around to Run Your Life!

Jana — my beautiful daughter — was truly one of the more pleasant surprises of my life. Coming along when I was 39, she amazed us all from the moment the rabbit died. (This was long before that newfangled "pee on a stick" method of figuring out you were pregnant!)

Now in her early 30s, she's happily married, a terrific mother, a great cook and my toughest critic. She has a natural wit, her mother's survivor instinct, and a heart as big as a clown's shoes! But perhaps what I appreciate most about Jana is the fact that she keeps me so young! After all, if it weren't for Jana — also known as Jay Bird, JJ or just plain Jay — I wouldn't know:

- That I can get a tan from a bottle.

- That the more wrinkles I have, the less blush I should use. (It won't be long before I have to even worry about buying the stuff!)

- That it's OK to wear a baseball cap while walking my dog (but only if the cap is pink).

- That it's "in" to have the "messy look" when it comes to my hair.

- That any perfume I wear — and any clothes, as well — should have been purchased in this century.

She does her darndest to keep me as young and trendy as possible. And believe me, some days that takes work!

Jana — in her up-front, candid way — keeps me in the moment, in style and in tune to what's "in!" This in-your-face attitude of hers may even have saved me from an early death.

When she was in high school (and if you've ever raised a teen, known a teen or been a teen, you know that *they* know everything!), she said two words that saved my life.

Here's the scene: I was in my bedroom, admiring a "major purchase" I had indulged in — a beautiful sweater — and I could hardly wait for Jana to get home from school so I could show it to her. When she came home, I excitedly said:

"Guess what? I bought something new today! Come see it! Come on!" I grabbed her hand and led her to the bedroom, where on the bed was this gorgeous sweater that I fell in love with, and that I was sure my daughter would, too.

As I admired it, I asked, "do you like it?"

"Yeah, it's pretty, Mom," she said in a less-than-enthusiastic tone. She turned and started to walk away.

"Well, Jana, you can wear it, too," I said, smiling and trying to get her to show some enthusiasm.

My daughter, Jana, (Jay!) and her beautiful family — Chad, baby Cambree and son Caden

"No, that's OK."

This threw me. "You don't want to wear it? Why not?" I asked as she started to walk out of the room.

She turned on her heels, took a deep breath, squared her shoulders, gathered all her emotional strength and replied with the verbal equivalent of a brick between the eyes: "Because it STINKS, Mom…. Because _YOU STINK_!"

"Wha…. What do you mean?" I asked, dumbfounded.

"YOU STINK, MOM," she bellowed, a second time, the gates overflowing now that she'd finally had the courage to tell me exactly what she thought of my smoking habit.

My eyes welled up and I started to cry. "How can you _say_ that to your mother?"

"It's the truth, Mom. You stink. The house stinks. The car stinks. _I_ stink! I go to school and the kids can smell me."

Words hurt. And sometimes, hurtful words help.

Until that very moment, I had no idea how much my smoking affected my daughter and other people in my life. But boy, did she make me see how my rotten habit was impacting everyone around me — especially my loved ones.

So I threw out my cigarettes that day and haven't smoked since. If it would help anyone else conquer that nasty habit, I share this with you:

YOU STINK!

*Do we laugh because
we're happy, or are we
happy because we laugh?*

19
No Strangers, Just Friends
I Haven't Yet Met

One "Embarrassing Mom Habit" Jay hasn't been able to break me of is my desire to strike up a conversation with anyone — and anything — at any given moment.

I speak to total strangers. I ask their name and call them by it. Whether at the grocery store or garage sale or soccer game, I have to connect with the people around me!

If I'm in the right mood, I'll even talk to the candy racks and magazines. Reading a tabloid headline or two out loud is a great conversation starter with almost anyone — except my daughter, who, if she's along with me at the time, is by this point pretending that she doesn't know me.

I do things that would embarrass anybody ... anybody except me! That's how I have fun. And that's how I make sure my daughter is 10 steps ahead of or behind me, alternately denying she's related to me or telling me what *not* to do.

Yes, Jay challenges me and holds me to a high standard. But she also brings so much joy!

I loved watching her as she started showing dogs when she was about 10 years old, following in the footsteps of her mother, father and big brothers. She took Eric's miniature schnauzer, Ego, into the ring and won her share of awards, just as her brothers had done with their dogs. That experience with dog training is serving her well to this day — after all, she has two kids and a husband to raise!

Having raised what I consider three pretty wonderful children, I firmly believe that every pre-teen and teen-ager needs to excel at something. And when it came to Jana, she excelled at roller skating and playing the flute. However, any dreams Dwight and I may have shared of having the world's first professional roller-skating flautist were sadly not to be. Like most youngsters, she lost interest ... and discovered a new interest: *boys!*

It's a joy to tell you that my daughter eventually found her knight in shining armor ... although instead of armor, he was wearing camouflage.

Dwight and I couldn't have hand-picked a better guy for Jana than Chad. He was a hard-working Iowa boy, an Eagle

Scout, sergeant in the United States Army, graduate of Iowa State University ... heck, he was even a Lutheran!

And they found each other ... over the Internet!

Chad and Jana married and lived for a year in Hawaii, where he was stationed. After his discharge, they settled down ... just three blocks from my little house on Cypress Street!

Having served four years on active duty, followed by 3½ years as an inactive reservist, Chad entered the U.S. Army Reserve and was mobilized and deployed for 15 months to Iraq. Following his safe return, he's helping Jana raise their two children: Caden, who was 18 months old when his daddy went to Iraq, and Cambree, who arrived just 12 months after his return. As Jana likes to say, Cambree was a "welcome home" baby!

While Chad was gone, I saw my daughter take the reins of that household, doing everything necessary to keep Caden safe and "keep the home fires burning."

As you can imagine, she had some tough days. Can you picture dealing with "The Terrible Two's" all by yourself?

I still recall the two of us standing in her garage as we were carrying in groceries after a chaotic trip to the grocery store. In frustration, she said: "Mom, you don't know what it's like to have to do *all of this by yourself* with a 2-year-old!"

I turned to her and said sternly: "I *beg* your pardon. I DO know what it's like. And I not only had one little guy; I had two." And I thought at the time, but didn't add ... "with no sign of my husband *ever* coming home."

So she didn't get much sympathy from me! But in my heart, I couldn't have been prouder of my girl than during those months she managed with Chad deployed overseas. She did the finest job a woman could do. And she didn't ask much from me.

Mostly, she just wanted me to go to Wal-Mart with her.

To this day, you ask Caden what his mom's favorite store is and he'll say, "Wal-Mart!"

We had another important reason to frequent the local Wal-Mart store. At the entrance was a display honoring local service men and women — and we would always stop so Caden could spot the picture of his dad.

*Jana and baby Cambree,
my newest grandchild!*

*Jana and Chad's children,
Caden and Cambree*

> *"I've run out of sick days,*
> *so I'm calling in* dead.*"*

20
Choose to Love Your Job or
Choose a Different Job!

*I*f you don't love your job, you're wasting your life.

I first made that statement when speaking to a group of office
clinic managers early in my speaking career.

I never realized the impact my statement had until a few
months later, when my mail brought me a handwritten note
from a woman who had attended that program:

> *Dear Jenny,*
>
> *I attended the luncheon address you presented for office clinic managers a few weeks back. You told us all, "If you don't love your job ... you're wasting your life."*
>
> *What an impact that made on me!*
>
> *Your words gave me the courage to make a change! After umpteen years at a job I didn't enjoy, I turned in my notice and began looking for a new job. Thanks to you, I found one that I absolutely love and I've never been happier!*
>
> *Thank you, thank you, thank you. Please keep up your courageous, encouraging ways!*

I hope I've encouraged a few other folks out there to take a leap of faith.

I believe that loving your job has to be a choice, just like choosing to have a positive outlook every day. Those are two lessons I've definitely learned from experience.

I've been fortunate to actually love just about every job I've ever had — and I've had more jobs than most people. (No, I didn't collect pink slips ... believe it or not, it was my choice to move up and on!)

My first claim to fame was working as a soda jerk at Humphrey's Drug Store in Huron, S.D., owned by Ralph and Harriet Humphrey.

I'll never forget the day when Ralph's brother, Hubert, stopped in for a cool treat. Unfortunately for my customer, Sen. Hubert Humphrey, D-Minn. — as he was formally known at that time — sat directly in front of the phosphate dispenser.

"I'll have a chocolate soda," the senator told me with a vote-winning grin, and then went back to visiting intently with his brother.

I worked as smoothly as my shaking hands would allow, trying to simultaneously disappear out of shyness and nerves while also wanting to be as close as possible to this famous person and also impress my boss.

Into the soda glass I plopped first one, then another scoop of vanilla ice cream. Next came an indulgent squirt of choco-late — I was going to make this the best chocolate soda ever! — and then I moved to the phosphate dispenser for the final, effervescent touch.

I'm not sure if my eyes were on the senator or my hands were shaking or what, but what happened next, I don't think I'll ever forget.

As I tilted the phosphate dispensing lever toward me, to release the pressurized liquid, the stream didn't hit the inside of the glass, as it *should have.* No, on this historic occasion, it landed smack-dab on the middle of the ice cream mound, which proved to be a perfect launching pad.

You guessed it. The phosphate/ice cream/chocolate syrup mixture splattered everywhere but in the soda glass. And in this case, "everywhere" meant *all over the senator.*

The fine mist of the phosphate dissipated evenly, though, so it was more of a light spray application than a splash. To my relief, it was barely noticeable.

The senator didn't even blink an eye; he was so busy talking with his brother. And the conversation must have been intense, because his brother didn't even notice that the eyebrows that the senator was so expressively wagging up and down as he talked were now shellacked with a fresh coat of sticky soda spray.

I wish I could say that was the last sticky situation I found myself in because of my work! But I've put my foot in my mouth — so to speak — lots more times.

For instance, my first job out of nursing school took me to the practice of a busy OB/GYN doctor. This man was so popular that he kept two nurses busy from early morning. We also had to scrub in for all surgeries, sit with labor patients and help with deliveries, then spend the entire afternoon in the office assisting him with his patients. He often saw 45 to 50 patients within four hours.

This was at the time when estrogen therapy was just coming into its peak, and he wanted all his patients to have the benefit of it. That meant one to two intramuscular injections for each patient.

When you give an intramuscular injection, it has to be in deep tissue. The best place for that is usually the buttock. To make sure the two-inch needle is going DEEP into muscle, a nurse uses her thumb and index finger to gently pinch and "pouf" up the skin for the injection.

I'll never forget the day I was bent over, all poised to give nigh my 43rd shot for the day. I had prepped the area with alcohol, filled my syringe with the "gold" (that's what it was called those days), pinched the skin together with my thumb and forefinger.

I proceeded to plunge the needle directly into my own THUMB!

I can still hear that patient say: "Wow, you sure did a nice job, nurse ... I didn't feel a thing!"

Do YOU think I told her what I felt? I was too proud, too scared, too dumb, too embarrassed to let her know that her shot of the "gold" had missed its mark. I just smiled, accepted her compliment, and gave her a thumbs-up.

Another of my favorite jobs was as an Adult Health Occupations instructor for the community college. I would go to a healthcare facility and teach the course to their staff who were required to become certified in their skills.

One day I was teaching the medication course for certified nursing assistants who worked in nursing homes. I purposely made the course exceedingly difficult. While standing at the chalk board with my back to the class, I was writing as fast as I could, all the while talking about the material I was writing.

I started to hear snickers from my students. I kept right on writing but said, "You people had better pay attention. This is important and you will be tested on all of it."

The snickering continued.

"Class! This is important!" I said in my sternest voice. "You're going to need to know this information. You had better settle down."

I continued writing faster and faster, and the snickering grew louder and louder. People were all-out laughing!

Finally, I swung around, put my hands on my hips and said in a scolding voice: "WHAT'S GOING ON HERE? Don't you know you're going to have to know this material? This is no laughing matter!"

They appeared not to hear me. I turned to a girl in the front row and demanded with a rigid finger pointed an inch from her nose: "You tell me what is SO funny!"

She stopped laughing long enough to say, "Mrs. Herrick, we didn't know you had grown a *third 'boob'* in the middle of your back!"

My shoulder pad had slipped down the back of my blouse!

I've been a psych nurse (felt right at home!), an OB nurse (helped deliver a lot of little people), a jail nurse (quit that job before I got fired), a product educator for a large market-ing company (Dripride) and a USDA small animal inspector (puppy mills, exotic animal auctions, catteries, rabbitries, airline shipping of animals).

To this day, it's hard for me to enjoy going to a zoo, rodeo or circus because I know too much!

One type of nursing I never experienced but would have liked to was in the field of urology. I would have loved to have answered the phone: "Urology Department ... could you please hold?"

Another time, I worked as a volunteer coordinator, supervising pre-teens and teenagers at the hospital. Boy, I lived through some weird fads — for instance, I remember when girls would "tease" or "rat" their bangs to make their hair stand straight up — and then lacquer it in place with an entire can of Aqua Net. Thus, the famous Mall Bangs.

I also survived the era when boys wore their pants extremely low on their hips — so low sometimes, I held my breath thinking "I don't need to see that" and understood why they thought they looked "cool" — they had built-in air-conditioning down below! Those also were the days when teens would suggest that you "chill out" or "cool it, dude."

When working with teen-agers, it's important to have a sense of humor. I distinctly recall reading that the meaning of the word "humor" comes from the Latin word umor, which means to be flexible, to flow like water — that's where the phrase "go with the flow" originated — now that's cool.

The chef at a family-run restaurant had broken his leg and came into the insurance office to file a disability claim. As the insurance agent scanned the claim form, she did a double take. Under "Reason unable to work," the chef had written: "Can't stand to cook."

> *A man may make mistakes,*
> *but he isn't a failure until he*
> *starts blaming someone else.*

21
Never Too Old to Go Pro

*O*ut of the mouths of babes can come the wisest words.

If it weren't for words uttered by my niece, Marsi, I wouldn't have launched my umpteenth career as a motivational humorist. At least, I wouldn't be getting paid for it.

But a verbal nudge from Marsi gave me the courage to "go pro," for what I expect will be the last notch in my career belt — unless, of course, I decide to take up naked hang gliding in my nineties. How many tickets do you suppose I could sell for *that*?

Back to the launch of my speaking career:

It was the mid-1990s, and I had been speaking on a volunteer basis (translation: for FREE!) for several years, happily sharing my messages with church groups, women's clubs and anybody who would listen. With a few years of Toastmasters and a ton of real-life experience under my belt, I had an interesting story or two to tell!

I was having fun, getting better and better (or so I thought), and doing it all for free.

I was telling Marsi about my latest adventure and about the positive response my presentations seemed to bring from my audiences.

Marsi asked, "have you ever thought of becoming a professional speaker?"

"You know, I've thought about it," I told my niece. "But I think I'm too old."

"No, Aunt Jenny," she replied, "you're not too old. Go for it."

So I did.

Marsi did another nice thing for me that I'll always remember.

She had come to hear me speak in Des Moines, Iowa, along with her mother and father (my sister and her husband). They were way in the back of a room filled with 1,000 people, but having family there made all the difference to me — I could feel their love and support from across the sea of faces!

In my speech that day espousing the benefits of a positive attitude, I told my audience:

"I would love to have a bumper sticker that says: If you're not using your smile, it's like having a million dollars in the bank ... and no checkbook!"

Lo and behold, two weeks later came a big envelope. Inside? A personalized bumper sticker that said those exact words — a gift from my beloved niece, Marsi.

That proves that at least *one* person was listening to me that day!

Police were called to a
daycare where a 3-year-old
was resisting a rest.

22
Can You Come Out and Play?

Whatever happened to fun?

Once in my speaking career, I presented a program titled exactly that: "What Ever Happened to Fun?" Crayons, coloring books, bubble gum, jacks, paddle boards and a variety of gadgets popular so many years ago — actually some even before my time — were scattered across all of the banquet tables. Since my audience included people of all ages, I thought it would be fun to see who could blow the biggest bubble!

Picture a hundred or so men and women (some hadn't chewed gum in years!), chewing and puckering up their lips trying to blow bubbles for all they were worth.

Talk about your Kodak moments!

It's a pity people don't make time for fun! I believe some people have simply forgotten how to play! It's our choice if we stop having fun. Nobody has ever said: "Now look here, you've reached a certain age. From this day forward, you can no longer have FUN!"

Even a fake *smile can get the giggles going!*

Think back to some of your favorite things that you did for play as a child. Can you remember the silliness, the craziness . . the spontaneous, uncontrollable laughter you engaged in while playing? That kind of soul-cleansing belly laugh certainly doesn't have an age limit.

I vividly remember as a student nurse, sitting in our chapel that had been temporarily converted from a classroom at the "ungodly" (is that sacrilegious?) hour of 6:30 a.m. We weren't even half awake and it didn't take much for one of us to start giggling.

Sure enough, that trickled down the row until a half dozen or more of us were trying hard to stifle our laughter, which was nothing but an expression of our joy of being there!

Don't you *dare* tell that story to the chaplain!

---

*If at first you do succeed, try
not to look so shocked!*

23
Keep Talking, God, I'm Trying to Listen!

Laughter, and a well-developed sense of humor, can get us
through some painful moments in life.

Like the day I made my demo video to promote my speaking
business. Not that the actual videotaping process was painful — in fact, I barely wince at all when I watch it — but the
events leading up to it caused some significant discomfort.

The day before I was to make the video, I was wearing some
new sunglasses and apparently paying more attention to how
fashionable I looked than the pavement I was floating above.
I took a dive. Right onto the concrete.

My right side and shoulder took the brunt of the impact.
Being the martyr I am, I simply brushed myself off, used
a tissue to dab a little blood from my hand, and continued
into the hotel. After checking in, my assistant, Marge, and I
continued on to some power shopping and dinner.

Marge — a registered nurse, like myself — asked me
throughout our shopping and meal, "Are you sure you're
OK? You don't want to go to the emergency room?" I assured her all was well — not wanting to give in to the nagging feeling that maybe it wasn't, and not wanting to miss an
opportunity to power-shop.

My denial continued through a sleepless night. After all, I
couldn't be seriously hurt; I had worked too hard to get to
this point! I was paying a lot of money to be videotaped
and was counting on doing the best job I could. So I simply
popped a few ibuprofen that Marge pulled from her endless
supply of necessities and pulled the covers over my head.

Still, my assistant wouldn't let up. You've got to know a bit
about Marge. Along with being an RN, she's the most agree-
able, organized, easy-to-be-around person you could ever
meet. Miss Have Whatever You Need, she's come through
for me with everything from a needle and thread to a clean
pair of underwear. I've seen her do things with a stapler most
people couldn't even dream of! She can fix anything!

And she could tell from the pained look on my face that I
was in need of some fixing.

But I wouldn't listen to her, not even the next morning when
I came out of the shower trembling. I had the shivers, and
it wasn't from the water being too cold. I was dried off and

dressed, and still shaking. In response to Marge's concerned look and question: "You *sure* you don't want to go see a doctor?"

Marge and me —
hey, we clean up pretty well!

I responded with what I thought was a joke: "Aw, I'm fine. I'm shaking for one of two reasons. Either I'm really nervous … or I'm hemorrhaging internally. Either way, I'm taping my performance *today*."

I've heard that nurses and doctors make the worst patients. At that moment, I understood why: They just know too much. In my case, I think I knew I had done something more serious than bruise my shoulder. But I wouldn't give in; I wouldn't say "uncle." I had too much at stake.

But the pain I was denying actually disappeared the minute I walked onstage. As every speaker knows, once you're on that platform, nothing takes precedence over getting your message out there in the best way possible. Adrenaline is an amazing thing. I gave one of my best performances that day.

With my videotaped performance in the bag and a few more ibuprofen in my system, I drove Marge and myself the four hours home. But the nagging pain from my fall continued, and two days after returning home, I saw a doctor. The diagnosis? A lung contusion (translation: badly bruised lung) with bleeding. I really *had been* hemorrhaging internally!

So now, instead of saying, "go break a leg" to wish me luck for an upcoming show, Marge just tells me, "go bust a lung."

While in this case I gave a strong performance while suffering from a serious injury, I recall the time I gave one of my worst performances with a simple head cold. Trying to quiet my symptoms, I overmedicated. So there I stood, before the crowd, seeing double. I rambled. I repeated myself. I rambled. think everyone was looking forward to my shutting up and sitting down!

So I've survived sticking my own thumb with a needle and tripping on my ego and bruising a lung. You'd think I'd learn to seek medical attention sooner rather than later! But a Sunday walk into my church — St. Luke Lutheran in Sioux City — proved that lesson hadn't quite sunk in yet.

As I walked into church, I slipped on the ice and fell.

Talk about a way to get attention! Within moments I was surrounded by all these handsome men in suits and ties, gallantly helping me up, brushing off my coat and escorting me to my seat. Throughout the service, my daughter kept whispering to me: "Mom, are you OK?"

I assured her that yes, I was.

In fact, just to prove to her and all my chivalrous knights who had come to my rescue, I walked with nary a limp up for communion and back. Any usher who asked, "Jenny, are you OK?" got a smile and a "thank you, I'm just fine!"

This was also St. Luke's annual holiday dinner, so I walked downstairs with everyone else to indulge in the great food and ambiance. If I felt a twinge or two from my tumble, I hid it; I wasn't going to miss the turkey and all the trimmings!

After the dinner, I got home and called Marge for our afternoon at the community theatre. As I sat in her car, I said:

"Did you notice I'm walking a little gingerly?"

"Yeah, what happened?" she asked.

"I slipped and fell going into church today; do you suppose He is trying to tell me something?" I joked with my friend.

Unfortunately – OK, I mean fortunately – Marge is a bone nurse who works on the orthopedic floor at St. Luke's Regional Medical Center in Sioux City when she's not traveling with me for my speaking engagements. She's one *hip* nurse. And I do mean "hip," as in the body part.

She expressed her concern about getting my injury checked out, but once again, I ignored her, toughed out the walk into the theatre and to my seat and thoroughly enjoyed the production — except during intermission. When I stood to stretch, I could really feel the stiffness and bruising from my fall.

Still, it hadn't reached the point where I felt the need for a medical opinion.

That point came the next morning, after a rough night in which I wished and prayed for stronger bladder capacity so I didn't have to get up and walk — in pain — to the bathroom.

By morning, the pain was downright severe. It was time to say "Uncle." And "Aunt." And "Cousin," and the whole family tree!

I called the doctor and went in for an appointment.

The x-rays showed I'd been walking around for 24 hours on a broken hip. *What kind of idiot walks around on a broken hip?*

Thankfully, my doctor — a handsome middle-aged surgeon whom I'd never met before – told me: "Because you're so physically active and mentally alert, I tell you what; I'm not going to put any screws in that hip. I'm just going to tell you to stay off of it for eight to 12 weeks."

(After he said the words, "mentally alert," I looked him in the eyes and mouthed, "I looooove you!")

His prescription worked, and three months later, I was back to my old self. And during those three months, I managed to make three speaking engagements and hop — I mean, carefully board and unboard — a plane to San Francisco!

My point? Before these physical setbacks, I had known that a positive attitude and the ability to see "the funny" in everyday life had helped me through some emotional struggles over the years. Now I also had proof that the same recipe worked for physical pain as well.

Still, it's important to listen to your body. And when your body says "OUCH," do the smart thing and see your doctor.

> *Always remember that you're*
> *special and unique ... just*
> *like everybody else.*

24
Not the Sharpest Crayon, But I Am Pretty Colorful!

To this day, my life as a professional speaker continues to challenge me and sharpen my sense of humor. And it continues to teach me tons about human nature ... and myself.

I remember speaking before a hospital group in Council Bluffs, Iowa. Not knowing a soul there, and not having been told where to sit, I parked myself at the table closest to the lectern, which I soon learned was also reserved for three nuns who would be arriving late.

As I ate my salad and enjoyed the ambiance, three women

sat down and introduced themselves to me as Sister So-and-so, Sister This-and-That and Sister Whomever (not their real names, but you get the idea!).

Quick-witted as I like to think I am, I responded: "Oh, how lovely to meet you! I'm Sister Jenny."

"Nice to meet you, Sister Jenny," came their replies, and we continued to visit right up until the program — all the while with them assuming I was "one of them."

As the emcee began speaking, I listened intently as he introduced our speaker, Jenny Herrick. When it was time for this "mystery speaker" to make her appearance, I smoothed my outfit, looked over at the nuns, said "I've got to go now, ladies, but I've really enjoyed my time with you!" Then I pushed out my chair, stepped to the lectern, smiled as innocently as possible at the trio, and launched into my address.

I still can see their faces — and I am grateful that they took my little act as just that, an act. The trio grinned and laughed and looked back and forth at each other and at me, then sat back to enjoy the program.

I'd like to think that those three nuns kept smiling my way as I walked out, the truth of my deception long revealed. I trust that they forgave me for my innocent farce. And I also hope that they said a few "Hail Mary's" for me!

Another time, in order to get to know my audience before my presentation, I "worked the room" from the floor before doing so from the lectern. The setting featured a casual open bar. I put a towel around my waist for an apron, grabbed a note pad and pen and proceeded to take their drink orders.

I hope those people aren't still waiting for their drinks.

Often after I give a speech, people will approach me to chat and share funny stories or jokes and such. At one event, while I was still on the stage, visiting with

Sharing my red nose with a lady of the cloth

my audience after my show, as I had a line of people waiting to talk, one particularly well-dressed man pointed at me and said in an attention-getting voice: "I want to know your fee and availability."

Without missing a beat, I put my hand on my hip, looked at him with a come-hither grin and replied, in front of the gathering crowd:

"That depends on what you want…."

Turns out he was a doctor who hired me to fly to his hospital and speak two hours and fly back the same day.

One event that I don't hold favorably in my memory is when I spoke to a national guard unit in their actual hangar at the airport. What was so bad about that, you ask? Two words: Acoustics and alcohol.

Imagine what the acoustics in an airplane hangar would be like. Add in a free open bar at the back of the room and picture me trying to get my message across amid all the competition — acoustics, laughter at the bar. I felt like Jonah inside the whale, with my voice reverberating back ... and nobody but God listening to me. (I must add that the next day, I received a darling clown music box from the general, along with his apologies for the poor speaking accommodations.)

Another less-than-favorite moment came inside a pole building at the Cherokee County Fair. It was Women's Day at the fair and 105 degrees in the shade. I was a guest speaker, trying to hold my audience's attention. But I had competition.

Now I know why they call the wind "Mariah."

The wind has to be a woman. After all, on this particular Women's Day, she showed up with full force! Some women, they just *have* to be the center of attention!

The hot wind whipped through the pole barn and stirred up dust at the feet of the farm women perched on metal bleachers. These hardy, salt-of-the-earth women barely seemed to notice my friend, Mariah. Meanwhile, there I was, juggling a microphone in one hand, trying to keep track of scattering props with another hand, and watching from the corner of my eye as my assistant, Marge, desperately spread arms and elbows and even a foot or two across our display table.

To this day, I imagine copies of my flyer scattered throughout cornfields all over Cherokee County, Iowa.

And it's not like this wind was a cool, refreshing one. It was the type that set the sweat dripping down your face, the small of your back, the corner of your eyes. And here I was, trying to look professional!

Not that my audience noticed my dilemma, I suppose. After all, within a 10-foot radius of the tent, they could enjoy the sights of a little boy walking his dog to the 4H dog pavilion, the sounds of a farmer putt-putting his tractor across the road to bring a few hay bales to his livestock, and a man pounding down pole stakes to set up his display.

Eventually, thankfully, all eyes turned back my way — even those of the fellow on the tractor.

After all, I mentioned how windy it was. But did I also tell you that I had decided that warm day to wear a light, flowing, airy skirt?

Like I said, you really need your sense of humor in such conditions. As well as a big lack of modesty.

I don't know if I'll be doing any more county fairs for awhile. Unless they throw in free horseshoe paperweights and all the funnel cakes I can eat.

Unfortunately, I don't always leave my audiences laughing.

Once, after a group of clowns and I took part in a parade in Yankton, S.D., we stopped at a local restaurant — in clown persona — for lunch. We were having a great time, meeting and greeting and good-naturedly ribbing everyone – as clowns are known to do — before we all sat down to order.

I didn't even blink as I introduced myself to a table of very well-dressed people.

First, let me explain that my clown character, "Lottie-Da" (I got that name from a prostitute in a book I read once), tends to be a little outspoken — even more so than her alter-ego.

How exciting to meet communications guru Zig Ziglar!

So I leaned over to the table and say loudly, so all the restaurant can hear:

"Boy, aren't you folks all spiffed up? I bet you just came from a wedding!"

Chuckles all around me … except from the table of well-dressed folks. They didn't say a thing. They just looked at me, some with awkward grins; others with deadpan expressions.

I didn't press the issue. I just grinned at them, shrugged my shoulders and went on to the next table.

Come to find out later that the people were indeed dressed up for a church occasion — a funeral. I learned the hard way that you can put your foot in your mouth, even when you're wearing big, red, floppy shoes.

*When everything comes
your way, you're in the
wrong lane.*

25
Breaking the Language Barrier
With Laughter

I've always been a friendly person, but spending 12 days in
China with 44 other goofy people helped me to realize that
there truly are no strangers, just friends I haven't yet met.

My career as a healthcare provider — nurse, caring clown
and coordinator of junior hospital volunteers — spans five
decades of stories and faces. Some of my fondest memories
come from those 12 days in September 2000 as part of a Fun
Medicine Delegation to the Republic of China led by the
world-famous clown/physician, Dr. Patch Adams.

We left American soil dressed as clowns and stayed that way

almost exclusively until we returned a week and a half older and decades wiser. We traveled in costumes, greasepaint, oversized shoes and thick, colorful wigs throughout the days of 90 degrees and 90-percent humidity. And we shared giggles with thousands of persons from our host country — hoisting tiny children on our laps at orphanages, drawing and entertaining crowds in every public square and starting a conga line with residents at a home for the elderly.

The first night, our bus dropped us off at Tiananmen Square, a place I knew from 1989 when Chinese protesters faced off against military tanks to the inevitably saddening conclusion, all while news cameras rolled.

I stood on that exact same spot, wondering if I had what it would take to make a difference. Even though I was a graduate of two clown colleges and a member of this hand-picked clowning team, I felt inadequate. I was in a country where I didn't speak the language. They had no idea why we were there, who we were, or even what a clown was.

So I stood at this spot known worldwide for a horrific event, feeling quite inadequate.

Then the people came.

They swarmed around each clown, smiling and giggling while covering their mouths. Of course, we had no idea what they were saying. We did know that they looked ready to be entertained!

What to do? I'm no juggler. I'm not a magician! I don't play a musical instrument or ride a unicycle. What to do?

I quickly reached into my bag filled with assorted props and my hand closed on my two-foot-long, bright yellow, giant toothbrush.

Immediately upon seeing the toothbrush, my audience giggled and laughed and pointed. So far, so good. But what next?

So I grinned, jutted my head out, bared my teeth as widely as I could, and pretended to be brushing my teeth.

Well, that definitely caused them to crack up! So what did *they* do, besides laughing, giggling and carrying on? They stood in front of me baring *their* teeth so I could pretend to give each of them their own personal dental cleaning!

I was having fun, they were having fun, so why quit? So I proceeded to take that toothbrush and pretended to brush my red wig. Lo and behold, one by one, they stuck their beautiful shiny black head of hair in front of me, and I pretended to brush *their* hair.

They laughed so easily. The sound was wonderful. And I thought I definitely was on a roll! So, I couldn't quit now! So what do I do? Lifting up my left arm, I took my toothbrush, and pretended to be scrubbing my armpit. And you're not going to believe this! Here stood dozens of Chinese people, all patiently lined up, one arm over their head, as they waited their turn for me to pretend to scrub their underarm as well.

Hundreds of people were gathered around me and my fellow clowns, and we all were doing our own thing, pulling tricks out of our bags and our imaginations, to entertain these darling people. Suddenly, the language barrier didn't seem to matter. Here I was, on the other side of the world, sharing the universal language of laughter with my brothers and sisters.

So many faces! So much walking and dancing and smiling! So many opportunities to share our joy of life and our message that humor can be a great healer — all in a country where they seemed to have the "work ethic" down pat, but couldn't quite grasp the "play ethic."

The next 10 or 11 days weren't always filled with laughter. The days we visited the orphanages were unlike days any of us had ever experienced. I recall walking into a building filled with these absolutely precious China dolls, dressed in dancing tutus and ballet shoes. That black hair, those shining black eyes, that porcelain skin. And someone had carefully applied just enough blush on those little apple cheeks that you really thought you were looking at a Dresden China doll. We were sitting around the room, and these little children paraded out, danced for us and sang. And we were told that they would probably never go into a home of their own, because there were just too many of them.

So here we are, looking at these children, and the tears are rolling down every one of those 45 clowns' faces.

Most all of us had brought little gifts, handing them out to these precious children.

Through our translator, we explained to the executives of every facility we visited why we were there, and of Dr. Patch Adams' mission to educate people on the value and power of humor. I hope we accomplished our goal.

Here are some of my favorite photos from my trip to China:

Me and my young
Chinese fans!

My new Chinese friends give the
camera a "thumbs-up!"

At a home for the elderly in Beijing, I join in a conga line.
I'm the second in line that you can see, wearing a hat!

With giant toothbrush in hand, I pose for a photo opportunity with a young man in uniform

My clown alter-ego, Lottie-Da, with a sweet little girl at a Chinese orphanage

*A Nobel Peace Prize ... I'd
kill for one of those.*

26
Face to Face,
Halfway Across the World

During our Fun Medicine Delegation to China led by
Dr. Patch Adams, my clowning colleagues and I saw
lots of smiling faces and unforgettable landscapes and were
growing in confidence that our message about the value of
humor — no matter what your circumstances — was getting
through to these people.

Then came our visit to a hospice in Beijing. (In China,
they're not called "hospices;" they're called "homes for the
aged and dying.")

What a stark contrast: Forty-five brightly colored clowns

traipsing into this dark, primitive, cheerless building where people lay on thin mattresses in tiny cubicles of rooms, alone, waiting to die.

Me with famous clown/physician Dr. Patch Adams

After gathering in a group while Dr. Patch Adams explained our mission to the staff, we spread out to interact with our assigned patients, one on one.

I went into my assigned area as quietly as my bright red shoes would allow. I entered my patient's cubicle and approached the small, still figure on the cot. The elderly man lay quite still, covered in a wool blanket and wearing wool socks in the oppressive heat, hands folded across his chest. At first, I did what every good nurse does: an assessment. Squinting in the dark, windowless room, I measured his respirations, assessed his skin color. His breathing, while shallow, was consistent. His eyes were fully closed.

Then I switched into clown mode, reminding myself: "Jenny, you've come halfway across the world to spread some cheer … get to it!" My inner pep talk did little to boost my confidence; in this situation, my task seemed insurmountable.

I took a deep breath, walked up to him, leaned down, and, doing my best not to startle him, gently put my hand upon his hands, which were clasped on his chest.

Immediately — almost as if I had flipped an electric switch — his eyes FLEW open! The dark pupils locked onto mine. His surprised, searching eyes took me in — clown makeup, bright-colored wig, red nose and all — but his expression never changed. He lay there, completely deadpan (perhaps not the best choice of words in this circumstance), except for eyes that seemed to be searching for something — *anything!* — familiar in this totally foreign moment.

Can you *imagine* what was going through his mind?

Whatever his thoughts may have been, he didn't say a word.

I had no clue how to proceed. Here I was, graduate of two clown colleges and member of a hand-picked team charged with spreading a few smiles in this country of 1.3 billion people, and I couldn't figure out what to do for this one man.

I found myself turning not to my clown training, but my nurse's training.

Slowly, gently, I began stroking this man's weathered hands with my own, sharing some "touch therapy." I kept doing so for several minutes in the dark room. I smiled. Soon, I noticed that I had begun to hum. For some reason, the tune, "I Love a Parade," was lilting through my lips.

Still, my patient showed no change in expression. His face was emotionless, but his eyes had a *"where am I?"* look.

All of a sudden I noticed water on my hands. I furrowed my brow, wondering where the water could be coming from. Then I realized — it was coming from *me*. Sweat was dripping off my face like a leaky faucet. I knew that if I didn't get out of there — very soon — I would be on top of this man, passed out from heat exhaustion.

I wonder if his expression would have changed then?

Rather than wait around and find out, I began to step backward toward the door, giving a tiny farewell wave and smiling, until I was out of his sight.

To this day, I have no idea what kind of an impact I made on this patient. We exchanged not a word. All I did was administer a little touch therapy, a bit of off-key music therapy, plus *a lot* of hydrotherapy. In my heart, I have to believe that I reached him, even though he didn't seem to acknowledge it. I was satisfied. I had done the best I could.

If nothing else, at least I had provided a little dying man with a big distraction — and quite the story to tell his next visitor!

I'll never forget the sweet, warm people of China

*Aspire to inspire
before you expire.*

27
Then Came 9/11

My clowning friends and I, before we left China, agreed: "We must get together again!" Someone suggested, "How about a reunion a year from now?"

That sounded great! We were planning it, looking forward to reconnecting with our clowning friends and sharing how we had all taken the lessons we had learned in China and put them to use in our personal and professional lives.

We kept in touch via e-mail and relied on our e-group to maintain our personal connections and work out the details of the reunion plans.

Then came 9/11.

So much for a clown reunion.

Our plans had changed. However, one of our group who lived in New Jersey wrote: "We traveled halfway across the world to spread mirth aid; I think we're needed right here at home. Let me see what I can do."

She got the OK from New York City authorities to "bring on the clowns." She then readied her townhouse for lots of guests, their greasepaint and their big red shoes!

We'd be clowning at Ground Zero, barely two months after the terrorist attacks. However, we were told that we could come, provided that we concentrate our efforts on the rescue workers – police officers, fire fighters, construction workers, ambulance personnel and others.

Only 12 of us were able to commit to this Ground Zero Mirth Aid Mission. Among the 12 were myself and a clowning friend I had invited, Diane Paugh (also known as Sparkle the Clown) and her husband, Mike, who served as our official photographer.

You thought the millions of people in China threw us for a loop? That was nothing compared to visiting Ground Zero. We had no idea what to expect! Would the silliness of a clown be seen as disrespectful? Would we be accepted? Would we be able to make a positive difference? This was something that really took some prayer on our part — what would it be like to see clowns at Ground Zero?

But we had a mission, and wanted to do the best job we could. So we put our mission in God's hands, asking Him to help us achieve whatever He wanted us to in our visit.

Right off the bus and onto the streets of lower Manhattan, I walked up to the serious-looking, handsome young officer who was standing at attention, saving a parking spot for our bus. I reached out with a red nose destined for his face.

"Ma'am, I'm on duty," the young officer told me, thinking words could keep my alter-ego, Lottie-Da, away from her appointed duty.

"Yes, I know you are," I replied, not stopping my forward momentum, "but trust me, you *need* this!" Bossy, wasn't I? I still can't believe I didn't earn my first pair of heavy silver bracelets that day.

But my fellow clowns and I continued spreading smiles, red noses and more. We worked our way through the thick throngs of visitors, looking for the rescue workers. Thank goodness clowns wear bright-colored clothing and hot-pink wigs; that made it much easier to keep track of one another!

We constantly reached into our pockets for red noses (I had brought hundreds with me on the plane; can you imagine what the airport security inspector must have thought?). We also packed in water bottles and power bars, knowing this would be a long, challenging day, just a block from the ruins.

Among the food, water and noses were handmade tickets printed on bright paper that said: "This Ticket Entitles you to a Free Smile!" or "This Ticket Entitles You to a Free Hug!" … I remember obligingly taking mine from the clown who was sharing them, thinking, "Those macho rescue workers are not going to be wanting these little pieces of paper!"

Boy, was I wrong.

Throughout the day, we were directed to spots where rescue workers were known to be working, eating and resting. We handed out hundreds of noses, hugs and smiles.

As for the tickets? They were our best sellers! OK, we *gave* them away, but they were nearly as popular as our noses!

We had big, burly New York firemen asking for tickets for hugs and smiles. We had police officers whistling from squad cars, asking for "one of those little green tickets if you still got 'em."

Guess what? We ran out of the tickets for free hugs or smiles — that's how powerful they were!

Throughout the day, we stayed in lower Manhattan, giving nose transplants, singing, handing out tickets, high fives, thumbs up and doing our best to spread some smiles.

Making friends and sharing smiles at Ground Zero

As we walked through the crowds, not knowing what these folks were thinking when they saw a clown en-tourage, I began to understand that we

had made the right decision to come here. I suspected it as
I saw the looks on peoples' faces as they shook our hands
and gave us high-fives. One woman reached up to give me a
high-five, and in doing so, exclaimed enthusiastically, "God
bless you!"

Wow! That did it. I knew this is where we belonged at this
time. And just in case we forgot, the warmhearted folks of
New York reminded us often with their words: "Thank you
for coming! You're *just* what we need!"

Our confidence grew along with our smiles. At one point, a
clown let out a wolf whistle at a passing police car, and we
ran over and did nose transplants, right on the spot! Several
hours later, we heard a honk, looked over, and by golly, there
was the New York City squad car, with those two handsome
young policemen waving from inside, still wearing their red
noses, giving us a thumbs-up and grinning ear to ear.

Police cars did U-turns to come see us. They shouted
"thanks" over their squad car loudspeakers. I can't tell you
how many times we were hugged by total strangers.

Once, standing and looking toward the smoldering ruins,
another clown and I suddenly felt strong arms around our
waists. One big man, grabbing us both, told us in his thick
New York accent: "Thanks for comin'! My shop is right
there, and you dunno how nice it is to see somethin' like you
in front of my shop because I've been looking at THAT (the
ruins of the World Trade Center) for the last nine weeks."

Another time, a man came out of nowhere to embrace me
in a huge bear hug. Then he backed up at arms' length and
looked at me with his hands held over his heart, tears stream-

ing down his cheeks, "You Americans…. You Americans!"
We visited police precincts and fire houses, sharing red noses
and hugs and posing for photos. We heard story after heart-
wrenching story. One fire lieutenant said: "I love clowns. A
clown saved my daughter's life." He told us how his 4-year-
old daughter had needed heart surgery and had to blow into
the breathing machine to keep her lungs clear. She was afraid
to do so until a group of clowns (The Big Apple Circus
Clowns) came into the room with bubbles. She was soon
helping them make bubbles, which helped her lungs to clear.

How did we feel about our Ground Zero trip once it was behind us? Thankful, grateful, privileged. We met people from
all over the world. We were humbled by their stories, their
faith, their optimism and their smiles in the shadow of this
overwhelming tragedy. I know that we left so much undone,
but at least we were able to provide a few needed moments
of diversion, humor therapy, stress relief, compassion and
love. And hundreds and hundreds of red, foam noses.

We learned a lot in
those 48 hours at
Ground Zero — most
importantly, perhaps,
that we should never,
ever, underestimate
the value of a clown.
I'll never hear the
song, "Bring on the
Clowns" again with-
out realizing just
how great clowns
really are!

*Me and pal Diane "Sparkle"
Paugh with an NYPD officer*

*I was taught to respect my
elders, but it keeps getting
harder to find one.*

28

Don't Worry, Caden. I Will!

Name tags? I've worn a few. Soda jerk. Wife. Clown.
Wife. Widow. Wife again. Mom. Survivor. Horsewoman. Step mom. Registered Nurse. My favorite? "Grandma."

I am a grandmother a number of times over, and proud as
can be of every one of them! Some are two-legged, and some
are four-legged, and I love them all to pieces.

Kirk has two gorgeous grown daughters, Tara and Trista, and
one "tall drink of water" of a son, Austin. Trista has a sweet
daughter, Lauren. Guess that makes me a "great" Grandma!

Eric and his wife, Sandi, have two beautiful Golden Retrievers, Bullet and Jenny (why yes, she *is* named after me! I wish

I was everything she was. She is the friendliest, sweetest dog you'll ever meet! And can she *swim*!).

And my daughter Jana and her husband, Chad, are responsible for the latest additions to my brood of beloved grandchildren: Caden, 4 and Cambree, 9 months.

Just as Art Linkletter says: "Kids say the darndest things." I am reminded of this every time Caden comes over for some quality "Grandma Time."

Since he recently became a big brother, I figured Caden was ready for a little more responsibility. I brought him downstairs where I keep more than 250 dog figurines. I've collected these miniatures over the years and received many as gifts, so each one carries a special memory or two.

Caden and I were admiring the shiny little pooches and I was gently dusting them when he said: "I like this one, Grandma," his small finger coming within an inch — but not daring to touch — one of the more adorable little figurines.

"I like this one, too," he said, his finger carefully moving to — but not quite touching — another keeper.

I figured he was old enough to help me with my cleaning ritual, so I carefully handed him one. This was a *big deal,* since I'd never before allowed him to touch my collection. "Be careful, these dogs mean a lot to Grandma," I told him, almost unnecessarily, as he gingerly — almost reverently — held and inspected each one.

"Grandma, I *really* like this one," he said, carefully turning the face of his latest favorite toward mine.

Caden and Roxy, two of my
favorite people

"Don't worry, Caden," I said in what I thought would be a reassuring note. "You don't have to pick a favorite. When Grandma dies, you can have them *all*."

His little face paused and his lips pursed together in thought. He looked up at me with his big blue eyes. "When you *die,* Grandma?" he said, slowly backing away.

"Yup, when I die," I said, matter-of-factly.

"Grandma," he said, a gravely serious look on his small face. "*You* gotta eat your *vegetables*."

Nice to know that I'm still his favorite old dog.

Eric and Sandy with my
namesake, Jenny, and Bullet

Me and my "tall drink of
water" of a grandson, Austin

Me and
Cambree

Trista, me (holding Lauren),
Kirk and Tara

Kirk with fiance, Debbie

L-R: Kirk, Caden, Jay, me
and Eric, being goofy!

"We are all here for a spell; get all the good laughs you can."
— Will Rogers

29
Hey, It's My Funeral

When I do go, I'm going big!

I've already told my children that when I die, my wishes are to be cremated — with my red nose positioned cavalierly upon my real one. No fancy urn for me! I've told them to bring a paper cup or coffee can to my memorial service so they can divvy up my ashes to do with whatever they wish!

This is going to be the best party I've ever thrown!

No sad sacks or long faces allowed. Just lots of uplifting, joy-filled music; a clown honor guard (all my clowny friends have been pre-warned and are actually looking forward to it, darn them!); some four-legged loved ones (I haven't gotten church approval for that one quite yet) and lots of great stories … all about me! It's my funeral, after all!

No tears allowed, thank you, unless they're tears of laughter.

Yep, my funeral is going to be one that folks talk about for years. It's going to be so much fun, I wish I could be there … oh wait a minute …. I *will* be!

I just hope this bang-up party's not going to be too soon. I wonder if my tombstone will say: "She Died Laughing"? What a way to go!

Me, as "Lottie-Da," and Roxy, ready to head out and spread some smiles!

It's not the load that breaks you down; it's the way you carry it.

30
A Few Last Thoughts Before I Pull Over and Let You Out...

People who know me also know that I never leave home without my red nose.

I've been known to put it on while waiting at a stoplight. I look to the left, wave and grin. I look to the right, grin and wave. I give a thumbs-up. Most times I get a wave or a smile back. Sometimes I just get the smell of exhaust as the folks hit the gas to get away from the strange, overly friendly, gray-haired lady with the sponge on the end of her schnozz.

I've been known to be a bit of a rebel. In fact, I've even forgotten my seat belt once or twice! If I happen to see a law enforcement officer coming in my direction, I grab the nose and don it simultaneously as I'm attempting to clandestinely snap my seat belt into place, waving as the officer drives by. (I think that most times the officer is a little afraid to stop!)

In the grocery checkout line? I put on my nose, or my equally appealing giant red wax lips (you remember, they used to cost 5 cents and we'd actually *chew* them for entertainment when we were kids!). Never fails, my line seems to move faster than any of the others!

The older I get, the more risks I take … what have I got to lose? I encourage you to consider taking more risks when it comes to having fun and enjoying each and every moment.

Give yourself permission to enjoy yourself! Laugh out loud. Act child-like. Grin from ear to ear. There's no better time than right now to begin! After all, why not choose today to:

- ✔ Wear that "good blouse" to eat ribs or that lovely lace nightgown you've been saving for a special occasion?

- ✔ Buy flowers for yourself? Why not really indulge and order a dozen roses … and give the bill to your boss?

- ✔ Call in "well" to work? (The next nice day, call work and say, "This is a great day, and I'm calling in well! See you bright and early tomorrow!" Now *that's* a risk!)

- ✔ Talk to other people in an elevator? The more crowded, the better!

- ✔ Play cards, kick the can, freeze tag, Annie-Annie-Over or duck-duck-goose (although for this last one, you may want to sit on chairs instead of the ground!)?

✔ Stop keeping score — in games and in life? Do you know that it's been proven that people who play a game where they don't keep score have a lot more fun than people who play a game where they do keep score?

✔ Splash on expensive cologne to walk the dog?

✔ Run through the sprinkler … on the way to work?

✔ Buy a pack of bubble gum and chew all five pieces at once?

✔ Pack a picnic for a favorite co-worker or friend and escape to the playground on your lunch hour and swing, swing, swing?

✔ Drive out to the country to look at the stars?

✔ Sneak into the neighbor's hot tub? Without a suit?

✔ Go to the library in search of a great adventure? (I remember walking to the library barefoot as my dog, Prince, carried my tennis shoes in his mouth, holding them by the shoestrings that tied them together. He'd wait in a relatively cool spot outside until I emerged with my treasures, then walk me back home, where I'd grab an apple and head for the nearest seat in front of the fan.) OK, I just realized that libraries have changed since I was a teen-ager. Along with your favorite books, pick up some DVDs or books on CD – preferably Red Skelton, Carol Burnett or Lucille Ball!

✔ Do those things you were too embarrassed or shy or self-conscious or "cool" to do when you were a teen-ager?

✔ Take your picture with a friend? Stop worrying about how old/fat/wrinkled/thin you look in photos, and start taking more photos of yourself in fun places!

✔ Buy yourself the softest, most decadent pillow and/or sheets you can afford?

✔ Take a vacation, even if you can't afford to go any-where? Spend a couple days volunteering for a great cause (may I suggest your local humane society?) inter-spersed with days of pure indulgence (hammock, lemon-ade and lazy afternoon, anyone?).

✔ Realize that not only has God put good people in your life — God has put *you* in the lives of other people for a purpose, too? Why not get off the couch, out of the office or away from those self-consuming tasks! Take the time to share your smile, your talents, your banana bread or whatever it is that makes you special?

Finally, when you're down and out, how about doing some-thing for someone else? Nothing boosts your mood and helps you forget your troubles like looking a friend in the eye and sharing a special moment! That reminds me, I need to go visit my friend, Hazel. So it's time to wrap up this book and get on to more important things….

I hope I've given you some laughs, some encouragement and some courage to seek out humor and fun in your everyday life. After all, life is too short to be taken so seriously! While we're here, it's our choice how we're going to spend every minute of this existence.

I say, let's spend it laughing!

JENNY HERRICK, JULY 7, 2007

Jenny Herrick believes you should laugh heartily and often — not just for the heck of it, for the health of it! Living proof that a sense of humor can buoy you through life's toughest challenges, Jenny enjoys sharing her message as a full-time speaker, professional clown and author.

A native of Watertown, S.D. and lifelong Midwesterner, Jenny is a graduate of the Lutheran School of Nursing (Sioux City, Iowa), Westmar University (Le Mars, Iowa), Clown College (University of Wisconsin-LaCrosse) and a Certified Laughter Leader (World Laughter Tour, Inc., Columbus, Ohio).

She has traveled to Ground Zero as a clown to provide "mirth aid" to rescue workers, joined a Fun Medicine Delegation to China with Dr. Patch Adams and started a Caring Clown Troupe at her local hospital. She trained dogs to win top awards in the ring and bring comfort as pet therapy canines. She is a Certified Laughter Leader and member of the National Speakers Association, Toastmasters International, Clowns of America International, Secret Society of Happy People, National Association for Self-Esteem, and one of the newest members of the Spirit of Women Speakers Bureau!

This book is her first venture into publishing, and she's looking forward to more! Let her know what you think!
E-mail her at *laughwithjenny@aol.com* or write her at:
All Kidding Aside, 2829 S. Cypress, Sioux City, IA, 51106
Check out her website, too at: www.allkiddingaside.biz

Kathy Hoeschen Massey is a freelance writer, photographer and copy editor. Originally from Alexandria, Minn., she has called Sioux City, Iowa home since 1984. When not collaborating with Jenny on her latest project, she works as church administrator at Redeemer Lutheran Church. She and husband, Ted, have two daughters, Katelyn and Courtney.